PRAISE FOR
The Marathon Salesperson

It was my pleasure and privilege to know and work with Rodolfo Subieta in the past, and I continue to learn from his insights into customer relationships. His book is a step beyond the three P's (Product, Price, and Promotion) of selling, into the more important aspects of establishing and maintaining the relationships that lead to ongoing sales. His organic approach to relationship building will benefit the reader in both professional and personal interactions.

—Sid Funk
Senior Director – Business Development
Massey Services

I really liked the six principles presented in the book. It was refreshing to see knowledge from fields such as physics, anthropology, and biology brought to bear in a book about sales. The eclectic references kept my attention while not distracting from the book's main principles. Hardnosed business types might scratch their heads at it, but that's good if it impacts the reverence often paid to dog-eat-dog competition debunked in the Fifth Principle—such competitive behavior leaves all of us poorer. I also liked the broadening of love in the Second Principle to include so much that is important in effective customer relations.

—Joe Reedholm
Owner and Entrepreneur
Reedholm Instruments, Inc.

I like the informal style and mix of personal anecdotes and authoritative citations. It is an easy read, making it a great candidate for a quick and helpful primer on selling.

—Dr. Richard Downes
Independent Researcher and Consultant
Former Sales Director for Latin American and
Caribbean, Detecom

The Marathon Salesperson includes Rodolfo Subieta's thoughtful reflections on what can help salespeople become even more successful. He lays an excellent framework for the selling process, reinforcing the importance of deeply understanding a customer's needs and wants, which is critical for a long-term partnership with that client. Honesty, drive, passion, and compassion are key elements he discusses and expands on in detail. As you will see, Subieta cares about the science and philosophy behind selling, building strong relationships, rebuilding bruised or broken relationships, and also knowing when to say no. This book offers a unique and colorful approach to the universe of selling.

—Bruce Jacobs
Sales Manager
Teleos Ag Solutions

THE MARATHON SALESPERSON

PRINCIPLES FROM HISTORY, SCIENCE, AND
NATURE ON HOW TO DEVELOP AND MAINTAIN
SALES RELATIONSHIPS FOR THE LONG RUN

Rodolfo E. Subieta

New Harbor Press
RAPID CITY, SD

Subieta/New Harbor Press
1601 Mt. Rushmore Rd, Ste 3288
Rapid City, SD 57701
www.NewHarborPress.com

Ordering Information:
Quantity sales. Special discounts are available on quantity purchases by corporations, associations, and others. For details, contact the "Special Sales Department" at the address above.

The Marathon Salesperson / Rodolfo E. Subieta. -- 1st ed.
ISBN 978-1-63357-235-5

Contents

ACKNOWLEDGMENTS

I would like to express my heartfelt gratitude to the following people who contributed directly and indirectly to this book's coming to fruition:

To my friend, former colleague and veteran salesman Sid Funk. This book had its origins in a collaborative workshop we both developed to train younger salespeople within our company at Dow AgroSciences. Sid's contributions to the workshop and, hence, to this book were not only material but inspirational. Reflecting on our knowledge and combined experience of dozens of years of building business relationships, we were able to extract the "golden nuggets" that went into the workshop and that are now part of this book.

To Phil Howard, my former district sales manager, for encouraging the creation of the original workshop; and to Janet Rowley and Nikki Hall for trustingly requesting that Sid and I present the workshop to their respective sales districts, thus providing us with the opportunity to try the principles in real time.

To Marcie Downing and Linda Fogle, also former colleagues, for kindly sharing their experiences and wisdom on how to deal effectively with the special challenges that women encounter in their business careers.

Along those lines, I am lovingly grateful to my daughters Monica, Erika, Karina, and Krystina for sharing with me their professional successes as well as their struggles. They are an inspiration to me and continue to teach me the meaning of fatherhood.

To my dear friends and former customers Al Bartlett (RIP), L.E. "Corky" Melass, and Alex Napoles Sr., who were an inspiration for writing the Second Principle of this book.

To Norman Goldenberg, a former customer, who at the start of my sales career gave me the opportunity to follow one of his working crews and to temporarily become one of them. I learned invaluable lessons that not only served me well through my career but later became part of this book. I'm also thankful to him for providing insightful suggestions for the completion of the manuscript.

To Liliana, my wife and life partner, for demonstrating throughout the years of our marriage that synergy, a concept I discuss extensively in this book, is indeed real and possible in a relationship. For granting me with infinite patience, the space and countless hours that it took to research, formulate the ideas, and write them down. For constantly watching my back and helping uncover my blind spots through my sales career.

To Dr. Larry I. Bone, wherever he may be, my former mentor and research supervisor at Dow Chemical, for helping me to see the bridges that connect science and spirituality, a concept I use in this book, and for believing that a scientist could become a successful salesman.

To Erika Subieta, a very special thanks, for taking the time to read the manuscript when it was still half-baked and temporarily paralyzed by writer's block; for seeing from a lawyer's perspective that the principles were applicable to professions other than sales. Her encouragement helped me more than she knows to come out of my writer's block.

A most cherished accomplishment of my sales career was the cocreation of the School of Structural Fumigation in Fort Lauderdale, FL, an example of cooperation among industry competitors that is discussed as a principle in this book. This collective achievement wouldn't have been possible without the involvement and continuous outpouring of energy, time, and resources from numerous unnamed people at Broward Community College and the University of Florida. I wish to thank them all and further acknowledge the following people for their unique contributions: mentor and founding director Doug Palmer; current director and promoter Renny Perez; cofounder, curriculum developer, and instructor Dr. Ellen Thoms; original instructor and University of Florida liaison Dr. Rudi Scheffrahn. Also, my gratitude to the following instructors—some of which my competitors—who year after year volunteered their time to make the Fumigation School happen: Sean Brantley, Dr. William Kern, Steve Niedzwiedzki, Eric Hobelmann, Jeff Edwards, Larry Riggs, and Jorge Moreno.

Last, but certainly not least, thanks to Bess Maher, my professional editor at Reedsy, who patiently collaborated with me to bring the manuscript into a coherent piece. With her suggestions, I was able to visualize and complete the book, one that could finally be published.

RELATIONSHIPS, ANCIENT PRINCIPLES, AND NATURAL LAWS

Selling is a multidimensional process. The first dimension includes what we sell: the product, the service, the idea, or the promise of a desired outcome. The second dimension includes how we sell: the marketing, the pricing, and sometimes the packaging. The third dimension involves the relationships that are established between sellers and buyers before, during, and after a sale occurs. These relationships need to be nurtured and sustained for sales transactions to occur repeatedly into the future. This book focuses on the third dimension, yet it cannot ignore the first two, for it would be foolish and deceitful to pretend that a shoddy "snake-oil" product or service can be sold sustainably just by having good customer relationships.

There are many parallels between running a successful marathon and achieving sustainable success as a salesperson in the long run. In both endeavors, we must undertake crucially important preparation; and in both, there are principles that govern our performance physically, mentally, and socially. Principles come in three main varieties: those that tell us what to do, those that tell us what not do (or what we shouldn't do), and those that simply state a truth.

How well we abide by, and master these principles determine our success or failure. In this book, I will present a foundational principle followed by a set of six enduring principles that build on one another and work together holistically at obtaining long-term, sustainable results. Each chapter is devoted to one of these principles. As a whole, they are designed to show you how to prepare for and then deal with the many facets and challenges you will face in your marathon sales journey.

Throughout the narrative of this book, you will see a recurrent theme: my quest to provide scientific, historical, and spiritual context—time-tested wisdom—to the principles presented. Let me relate the evolution of what gave birth to this three-dimensional approach.

Early in my life, I found that science could provide satisfying answers to most day-to-day questions. In fact, I discovered that science was an exquisite and precise tool that, when used methodically, could lead you to the understanding of basic fundamental truths. I also found scientific advances to be truly universal. A polio vaccine will protect a child from death or crippling existence whether the child is white, black, brown, or Inuit. And a light bulb will illuminate a person reading the Bible the same as one reading the Koran, or the *Wall Street Journal*. This led me to the pursuit and attainment of a degree of Bachelor of Science from college. After graduation, I started my career as a science teacher at a high school. Subsequently, I worked in cancer research and, later, in the field of biological purification of water. Later on, even when my career took me into the field of sales and marketing, I found that the majority of challenges I would encounter, could be solved or benefited by the use of a scientific approach. To this date, I am a science practitioner, and I continue to believe in science's ability to solve problems and in its humility.

"Humility? Scientists can be very arrogant people," you may rightfully observe. However, a true scientist can never profess to know the whole and absolute truth about anything. A scientific theory by definition is, and forever will be, incomplete and open to revision. A true scientist knows that his or her theory is only a model, an approximation of the truth, which in time must and will be replaced by a better approximation, and in turn this one too will be replaced by a better one still. And that is perfectly fine, because that's how science advances and polices itself, and how new technologies replace old ones. The emotional and intellectual reward of a scientist is that, for a moment, he or she is closer than anybody else to the understanding of a particular natural phenomenon.

Then, as I matured, I also realized that certain intangible but undeniable human characteristics, such as our universal yearning for fairness and justice or the concept of "trustworthiness," both crucially relevant to our interactions with other human beings—thus to salesmanship, could not be explained by the natural sciences alone; help from a different discipline was needed. Historical observation came to the rescue. It was historical observation that revealed unequivocally the fact that most scientific advances had been and can be used for both good and destructive purposes. Science itself is blindly unconcerned in this respect. It became almost an obsession of mine to find out if there was any remedy for this dichotomous condition. If we were to avert the destructive uses of science, we desperately needed a sort of "Collective Conscience Principle." I discovered that I was not alone in this quest. From time immemorial, sages and philosophers have observed and have wrestled with this issue. I suppose from the very first time that humans discovered that they could tie a sharp stone to a stick and make an axe that could help them to obtain food, but also to crack the skull of another human being. Thus, what I call a "Collective Conscience Principle" (CCP) slowly began to evolve and continues to evolve to guide humans on how to avert harmful or destructive uses of technology, and basically how to get along better with each other. On the surface, the principle hasn't been foolproof, and there were times in human history when it seemed that it failed miserably to avert widespread human destructiveness towards one another. Yet, time and time again, just like the mythological phoenix, it keeps rising from the ashes of destruction proclaiming that it's still alive and true.

Versions of this principle, referred collectively as the *Golden Rule*, can be found in almost every culture and religion. Some of the older versions of the Rule, dating back to about 500 BCE appear in Hinduism: "One should never do something to others that one would regard as an injury to one's own self," and in Confucianism: "What you do not wish for yourself, do not do to others." A more recent version appears in the New Testament: "Therefore all things whatsoever ye would that men should do to you, do ye even so to them." In a profession where human interaction is so important, the marathon salesperson cannot afford to ignore this ancient principle as the foundation of the other six that will be presented.

Selling itself is an ancient profession. From the beginning of recorded history, merchants brought products from faraway lands, through perilous long ocean voyages or across deserts and mountains. They would bring silk, spices, and fine garments for sale. Then, at some point, the concept of "salesmanship" evolved. Some of the merchants realized they could also bring news and discoveries to their clients—a glimpse or a taste of what was until then, unreachable or unknown to their customers. Medicines and scientific cures often travelled along the merchant routes. The most prosperous merchants learned and understood the importance of the third dimension of selling, the relationships with their buyers; as a result, their customers eagerly anticipated their arrival. These merchants were respected and appreciated.

Most enduring principles are based on natural laws. This relationship between principles and natural laws is easier to understand when we examine a fundamental natural law like gravity. From the beginning of time, gravity has affected anyone and anything that's on earth and will continue to do so with or without our consent or understanding. Even without an understanding of its cause, our ancestors observed the effects of gravity and then expressed the principle as "Everything that goes up must come down." Then, in the seventeenth century, some transcendental developments occurred. Thanks to the work of Sir Isaac Newton and others, we began to understand gravity as a force that all objects in the universe exerted. The more massive the object, the greater the force it exerted. Based on this new understanding, Newton postulated principles that explained and governed the motion of planets around stars and formulated equations to predict their trajectories.

Later, other scientists refined Newton's work. One of them, Albert Einstein, expanded our understanding of gravity as an effect of the distortion of the curvature of space-time—sort of a "dent" on the fabric of the universe—caused by a body. Einstein, in turn, formulated principles that quantified and predicted the motions of all bodies in the universe, the big and the infinitesimal, and the behavior of light.[1] And even though unanswered questions regarding gravity still remain, our evolving understanding of this natural law have produced extremely useful technologies that gave rise to airplanes, satellites, and space travel. Yet this is the same law that can still cause a person to fall from a third-floor balcony and crash into the pavement below.

On the other hand, the evolution of principles in the field of social sciences, which includes the art and science of selling, followed a somewhat less quantifiable path. In this field, humans passed along much of the knowledge on transactional human interactions in the form of proverbs. "You reap what you sow" is a familiar principle that is based on an observation of a natural law—sowing a seed and harvesting its fruit later—applied to human behavior. In other words, this principle makes predictions of what to expect in the future based on the actions we take in the present. It does a fairly good job at such predictions, yet it cannot be written as a mathematical equation. Why? Because there is an immensity of variables to consider, and it is significantly harder to conduct controlled research on people and societies than on physical objects.

To illustrate this point, let's consider one of Aesop's fables "The Boy Who Cried Wolf," written in the fifth century BCE, which deals with the consequences of lying.

It tells the story of a shepherd boy who out of boredom, or to amuse himself, cries "Wolf!" when there was none, just to see the villagers come out to help him. He does it a second time and the villagers again rush out to help him only to find out they have been deceived one more time. Several days later, a wolf actually shows up, and the boy desperately cries, "Wolf, wolf!" But this time the villagers, who have been fooled twice, didn't come to the boy's rescue and he suffers terrible losses. He plaintively asks the villagers why they would not help him (i.e., he questions his fellow villagers' lack of motivation to act in a way that could have saved him). The moral of the story—the principle—is given by the wise man of the village: "A liar will not be believed, even when he speaks the truth."

This ancient story and its underlying principle make a prediction of the future behavior or attitude to be expected from others as a result of one's actions in the present. It is a principle which basically establishes a direct correlation between a person's lying or telling the truth, and its impact on his or her "trustworthiness." The *New Oxford American Dictionary* defines *trustworthiness* as "the ability to be relied on as honest or truthful." As we go on interacting with different people in our lives, trustworthiness is that intangible attribute that we hold about a person, which *determines the strength of our willingness* to start interacting with him, to continue interacting with him, or to stop interacting at once. Many factors impact trustworthiness; it is a complex attribute, and it should be a career goal of a marathon salesperson to understand which factors have the greatest impact. Certainly, the principles that will be discussed in the following chapters are intrinsically good at increasing this attribute, but let's continue to examine the subject of lying and its effects.

As far as I can tell, no one has succeeded yet in expressing the correlation between trustworthiness and lying in a mathematical equation. Yet we know, based on historical observation, that both are inversely correlated (i.e., the value of a person's trustworthiness decreases with the number of lies he or she tells. In this respect, trustworthiness could be thought of as a personal bank account, and the lies would be withdrawals). But there is a caveat; for instance, the correlation cannot predict *with certainty* that lying twice will cause others not to believe you in the future at all, or that perhaps you can always get away with just one lie, like the boy who cried wolf did in the story. Moreover, within a large group of people—say in a large city—when is a person considered to be a "liar" by everyone?

Therein lies the challenge faced by social scientists: the enormity of variables in human interactions makes it very difficult to establish that an action will *always* cause a certain reaction, at all times and by all people. This leads some to believe that lying may not have bad consequences every time, or that it may even be profitable in some cases in the short term. This paradox was verbalized by President Lincoln—"Honest Abe"—with a refined principle of his own, when he said, "You can fool all the people some of the time and some of the people all the time, but you cannot fool all the people all the time." Lincoln, as a politician, was coming to terms with the *apparent* reality that lying or deceiving may not carry bad consequences in some cases. I say "apparent" because the consequences may not be immediate or visible, but newer evidence suggests that there are *always* consequences. Let's take a look at the evolution of this concept.

By the middle of the nineteenth century and the beginning of the twentieth century, a group of renowned thinkers and entrepreneurs, including Ralph Waldo Emerson, Andrew Carnegie, John D. Rockefeller, Jr., W. Clement Stone, Napoleon Hill, and Thomas Edison, among others, advanced our understanding of the correlation between our present behavior and future success or failure. The most fundamental concept advanced by these leaders was that not only our actions but also *the way we think* have predictable consequences. That the thoughts we allow and hold in our mind are to a great degree deterministic of our future was a hugely important development.

Napoleon Hill put it this way: "It may not be literally true that 'thoughts are things' but it is true that thoughts create things, and the things they create are striking duplicates of the thought-patterns from which they are fashioned."[2] He went on to postulate that one of the greatest powers we possess is the ability to control our own thoughts. To be fair, Hill's philosophy encountered criticism. Basically, the critics argued that if Hill's ideas were true, anyone could just "think himself or herself" out of poverty, illness, or conflict. However, I believe the criticism ignored one key component of Hill's philosophy: the crucial role the *subconscious mind* plays in determining our thought-patterns and, hence, our winning or losing behavior. Hill wrote extensively about the importance of *good habits* in the creation of a desirable reality from the subconscious.

Earlier, America's founding father Benjamin Franklin had put it in business language when he said, "Your net worth to the world is usually determined by what remains after your bad habits are subtracted from your good ones." Later, other contemporary authors and entrepreneurs, notably Stephen R. Covey, studied, researched, and concluded that habits can literally make you or break you. The good news is that we also possess the power to modify our habits, but there is no such thing as something for nothing, and we must be willing to pay the price that it takes to develop a set of winning habits and, even more difficult, *to ban from our subconscious* those deeply engrained habits that violate principles and produce negative results. I turn to the field of psychology to illustrate this point, referring back to the habit of lying and its consequences.

Previously, I implied that not just the telling of a lie, but also the *thinking* of a lie has predictable consequences. In other words, thinking deceitfully or truthfully leads to totally different outcomes in a person's life. And even though on the surface it may appear that some people are getting away and apparently benefitting from lying, we must understand that the *thinking* behind the lie creates an imbalance—a contradiction, a duality, a *compartmentalized split* in the person's mind— which eventually dooms the liar and his or her business and personal relationships. Bestselling author and psychiatrist M. Scott Peck explains it vividly in this way: "Compartmentalization is not the root of all evil; it is however the principal psychological mechanism of evil. Deprive an evil man of his capacity to compartmentalize, and he will be like a general without an army. Or better yet, he will undergo a conversion to goodness—a conversion to integrity."[3]

This brings to light another ancient principle: "No one can serve two masters." There is a biological natural law underlying this ancient principle, it relates to the conservation of energy. You see, the compartments created in the mind of a habitual liar are in constant conflict with each other. If consciously or unconsciously we get into a habit of creating questionable deals for our clients—Ponzi schemes being the most extreme—we might initially experience temporary benefits, but then, we will try to find justification for such behavior, "times are bad," "our competitors are doing it too," "I'm looking out for number one," "my customers don't really care." This constant search for justification not only uses a lot of energy, but it also reinforces the habit; in other words, we may start believing our own false narrative. But like keeping multiple sets of accounting books, the energy required to maintain these constantly conflicting factions is prohibitively large in the long run. A marathon runner who neglects the importance of energy procurement and maintenance eventually "hits the wall." In sales, the equivalent is a "burnout."

The habit will take its toll in terms of decreasing performance, leading to strained relationships and, eventually, even to a total collapse of our capacity to produce.

As you can see, the importance of understanding the concept of *trustworthiness* and all the factors that increase or decrease its value cannot be overstated.

This brings me to another influential thinker and author who I've already mentioned. I am grateful to Stephen Covey, who was a pioneer in the application of *principle-based behavior to* our private lives and to our public and business interactions. Many of the concepts presented in this book evolved from his work and from my own understating of the principles he formulated. In his seminal book, *The 7 Habits of Highly Effective People*, he explains that principles are fundamental truths. They remain unchangeable even though our understating of them may change over time. They do not seek our approval. We can ignore them at our own peril[4].

In this introduction, I have presented some basic, preliminary concepts and universal principles that should be considered as a foundation for what comes next. In the chapters that follow,

I will apply six main key principles to the field of sales, especially "marathon" sales. Each chapter will be dedicated to the discussion of one of these six principles. The concepts I will present may occasionally seem counterintuitive. Running a marathon requires different training, energy conservation, maintenance, and even a different state of mind than running a 5K race. Likewise, the development and maintenance of long-term business relationships is a different type of selling. It requires us to think and behave in ways that sometimes appear counterproductive, that even seem to go against the grain of what a salesperson is supposed to do: to generate profit from every sale. Yet consider for a moment how the throwing of seeds on a plowed field, a seemingly unprofitable act in the short term, which occurred to an ancient hunter-gatherer ancestor of ours, resulted in an immensely profitable harvest a few months later and a sustainable way of producing food. The understanding of this natural law and the subsequent formulation of principles based on this law gave rise to agriculture and civilization. In a similar way, the marathon salesperson must act according to principles that guarantee long-term success, not just short-term profit.

If at first you may find some of the ideas in this book surprising, some too simplistic, and some even preposterous, I ask that you give the ideas a chance, and I hope that you apply them. It is in their application—or sowing—that you will find they are true indeed and that they give good fruit in the long run.

It is often said that we all are salespersons at one time or another. Thus, even if you are not a professional salesperson, you will find that the principles we will discuss are universal and apply to every walk of life.

CHAPTER 1

PREPARING FOR THE LONG RUN

One of the most important and ageless secrets of life that I had to learn, with pain and tears, is that you cannot even begin to turn a hopelessly bruised and defeated existence around or jump off that dreary treadmill so far as your job and career are concerned or move off that financial dead end that seems to have doomed you to failure and low self-esteem until you appreciate the assets you already possess.

—Og Mandino

Imagine a thirty-five-year-old alcoholic who has lost his job, his family, and even his desire to live. He contemplates suicide by spending his last thirty dollars buying a gun from a pawnshop. But by his own admission, he lacks the courage to even kill himself. Yes, this is the same person who later became the editor of a successful magazine and the author of one of the most influential books of the twentieth century in the field of sales.

I read *The Greatest Salesman in the World* by Augustine "Og" Mandino II when I started my own sales career, and since then, I have bought dozens of copies of this wonderful little book to give to friends and colleagues. But it is in a later book[5], where Mandino shares the "rules" he followed to bring about his own redemption and eventual success. Sure, it is also possible that he got lucky, that he was in the right place at the right time, and that he got crucial help from the right people.

All of the above is possible, but the principles he followed seem to be common threads that run through the fabric of life stories of other successful people as well. Could it be that one positive action inevitably leads to another and then to another and then to a cascade of positive manifestations?

The first step or "rule" revealed and followed by Mandino is crucial preparation for the long run. It is really an ancient principle, and I must warn all aspiring salespeople and readers of this book that without mastering it first, the chances of having a successful marathon career in sales will severely diminish.

The First Principle: Count Your Blessings

The First Principle, "Count your blessings," is deceivingly simple. Yet hidden within these three words is the time-tested secret and the first step that leads toward prosperity in any stage of life. That is why it is also the preliminary training that we must learn and undertake in long-term selling and relationship building.

The word *blessing* may sound religious to some readers, and perhaps through years of repetition and misuse may have lost its true meaning. Theologian–anthropologist Kelly Isola provides a most insightful metaphor of what "blessing" encompasses. She says, "Interestingly, the word shares its origins with the word *blood*.

To understand blessing is to know it is an invisible, cosmic bloodstream pulsating through the universe."[6]

If we want to translate "Count your blessings" using more secular words, we could restate the principle as follows:

With a Grateful Mind, identify and quantify the resources that are constantly coming to you.

In the end, we can only build new things by utilizing *what's available to us,* or in broad terms, *what's around us.* In marketing and selling "what's around us" is the *field of opportunities.* To prosper, we must *convert* these opportunities into their physical form: sales revenue, leads, and goodwill. As we shall see later, we are not creating things from nothing, but transforming one form of thing into another. Let's take a closer look at this conversion process.

Matter and Energy

In scientific terms, what is around us is matter and energy. Most of us are familiar with Einstein's famous equation $E=mc^2$ that established the interchangeability of matter and energy. The process described and quantified by

Einstein's equation is an operating universal principle. Certainly, we see its workings in the way plants convert solar energy and a few nutrients extracted from the soil and air into plant tissue. The reverse process, and perhaps a more dramatic proof, is the production of vast quantities of energy by atomic plants from relatively small quantities of matter.

Even when we feel most isolated, in the darkest moments of our loneliness, we are not really alone. We do not and cannot live in a vacuum. Vast amounts of energy are "pulsating through the universe," as Isola observes, coming to us and literarily surrounding us at all times. It is the same in the business world. When we feel we have no opportunities, no chance of growth, we must remember that vast amounts of energy are pulsating through the universe and we need only to become attuned to them. The act of "counting our blessings" could be thought of as becoming aware of the energy that is around us and coming to us in various forms—some, as said earlier, in the form of opportunities. Examined in this light, missing opportunities occurs mostly as a result of being unaware or unable to utilize a particular form of energy in most cases due to our minds not being properly tuned into it. That's where the Grateful Mind comes into play.

The Grateful Mind

Why must we do the accounting of our potential opportunities with a Grateful Mind? Perhaps the results of a research study conducted by a team of social scientists on ex-convict recidivism will illustrate the point. The scientists wanted to find out the reasons that led one group of ex-convicts to straighten out their lives and become productive individuals after being released from prison, as opposed to another group that invariably fell back into the same pattern of behavior that caused them to be imprisoned in the first place.

The researchers were able to identify one common element in the first group of people: It was that every person had taken the time to deeply look inside himself or herself and came up with a Personal Talent Inventory (PTI). This was a transformational step according to the ex-convicts' own accounts. While the second group continued to focus on past injustices, mistreatment, and lack of opportunity in the outside world, the first group actually started focusing on their talents, i.e., the tools they had to work with. As hard as it was for most of them to realize initially, they did have things they could be grateful for. Most of them cried while going through this introspection. Imagine husky, tough men and women crying tears of recognition as they started uncovering the treasure buried deep inside their souls.

There is an old story about two shoe salesmen who went to a developing country to open up new territories. After their arrival, both conducted their preliminary market analysis. The first salesman sent a communication to the home office saying, "I am returning on the next flight. There is no market for shoes here. Everybody goes barefoot." The second salesman sent a message back to the home office a few weeks later. The message was: "I'm including a preliminary order for one hundred shoes—possibly more to follow. There is a vast potential. Nobody here has any type of footwear. *However, we may need to modify our existing inventory to better accommodate the requirements of these folks.*"

The Grateful Mind is what allows us to be truly receptive to the energy that's coming to us in the shape of opportunities. Gratefulness is the equivalent of tuning our own minds, so that instead of perceiving the blurred, ghost shadows from our past, all of a sudden we start perceiving coherent images—the eurekas, the bridges that connect our inner talents with the opportunities of the outside world.

The Quantification

Lastly, notice that the principle directs us to "count." It is not sufficient to just notice or recognize our blessings. It is in the quantification that we are able to see the real potential of what we can do, the magnitude of the blessings. In the process of counting and writing them down, something interesting happens, *we start taking ownership of the blessings.* Our perception begins to change from a glass half empty to a glass half full, then to a glass overflowing, and finally to a fountain.

"All things are created twice,"[7] explains Stephen Covey. This means we conceive of something first and then we create it. In selling, as in all walks of life, prosperity starts in our minds, with the first creation. Counting our blessings is part of that first creation.

Now, if you are in sales, you probably have a list of current customers. One of the first things a salesperson does when arriving in a new territory is to compile a detailed "situational analysis" of his or her customer base. This analysis must include sales figures, but if we apply the First Principle, and we start perceiving these customers as true *blessings*, we may discover that a customer not only can provide sales revenue but also other useful intangibles such as referrals, access to industry meetings and associations, information about what our competitors are offering, new trends and practices, assistance with new product testing, and even friendship.

Following is a practical exercise that applies the First Principle to your individual situation. Do this with every customer, even with the ones who seem difficult or are presently buying little.

First Practical Activity

1. Create a six-column spreadsheet in a computer or on a sheet of paper.
2. On the first column, write the name of the customer.
3. On the second column, write the tangible sales figures.

4. On the third column, write the intangible "blessings" the customer is already providing you or that he or she can potentially provide.
5. Leave the fourth, fifth, and sixth columns blank for now. You will use them in the next chapters.

As you perform this activity, you will be surprised to find out how your perception of your customers changes once you start viewing them in this multidimensional way. You will start seeing a different, augmented version of your customer base.

To summarize, the First Principle directs you to first become aware of your resources, your "assets," and then go further: Count them, enumerate them, single them out, recognize them, bring them out from the darkness. Then, own them, *take possession of them,* love them. You will see, that little by little, you will become comfortable with your blessings and will gain expertise on how they can be used to bring forth additional goods, even beyond the sales revenue. In other words, you will *see your blessings multiply.* And remember that running a marathon is accomplished with the body, but a lot of the preparation needed to stay in the long run—the planning—is done in the mind and by the mind.

CHAPTER 2

IN THE MATTER OF LOVE AND ENERGY

The conclusion is always the same: Love is the most powerful and still the most unknown energy of the world.
　　—Pierre Teilhard de Chardin

If a person wants to build a structure that will stand the rigors of time, he or she must put together building materials according to a plan or blueprint. The principle "Count your blessings" is the first step that allows us to create a blueprint, or in this case, a map of our sales territory with all its components, including sales revenue and intangible assets that customers and others can provide. It represents the first creation. But the second creation, putting together all these materials to achieve the desired result—say a beautiful house—will take the input of some form of human and/or mechanical energy. Sometimes we overlook the fact that the building of long-term, mutually beneficial *relationships* likewise requires input of energy.

The question is, what kind of energy is universally accepted, even yearned for, by every human being? What kind of energy has the power to transform for the better the way we perceive the world and the way we perceive others?

The Second Principle: Love Your Customers

The Second Principle is "Love your customers." If at first you find the wording of this principle a little woo-woo, we could also restate it as follows:

Proactively apply energy to relationships with the purpose of achieving enduring, social synergy with those who you want as long-term customers, and to achieve win-win results with them.

If you pause and read the above carefully, you will notice that it involves an action, that it is results-oriented, and that the results benefit both the buyer and seller. Also, notice how many words I had to use to restate "Love your Customers," this simple principle. As we all know, *love* is one of the most used and misused words in the English language. (For example, *love-fifteen* in tennis means a score of 0 to 1). But it's crucial that we look at love from a different perspective: Let's start by considering love as a form of social currency—that is, something we exchange, give, and receive. In fact, we could arguably say that love is one of the few—if not the only—forms of social currency that has universal appeal.

To be realistic, there are formidable roadblocks to the application of this principle. *Loving ain't easy*. In the field of sales, you have various options of how to relate with your customers. To name a few, you can halfway dislike them and force yourself to do business with them, you can take advantage of them, you can let *them* take advantage of you (some people confuse this with love), you can tolerate them, or you can actually *love* them. You will achieve different results depending on which option you choose to implement. However, if your aim is to become a marathon salesperson, and to achieve durable win-win relationships with your customers, the last option is pretty much the only one that will get you there. Everything else will fall short. So, let's dig into this thing called "love." Let's do a little study on it.

A Study on Love

To be effective, any learning curriculum has to be built step by step. If we fail at trigonometry, in all likelihood it is because we did not spend enough time to master algebra. Likewise, it is very difficult, if not impossible, to truly love what's indifferent or unknown to us. That's why mastering the First Principle, "Count your blessings," is such a foundational step before attempting to move into the Second Principle. As was said before, the development of a sense of ownership, a kinship with our blessings, occurs as a result of using the First Principle.

Another mental roadblock that often prevents us from applying the Second Principle is the misconception that we can only love those who are beautiful, normal, appealing, majestic, or that which gives us pleasure. The story of Dian Fossey, who spent thirteen years in a remote African forest among mountain gorillas, is a real-life example of the workings of the first and second principles. At first, Dr. Fossey like most people in the sixties, had misconceptions about gorillas. Most books and popular-culture articles of that time depicted gorillas as dangerous, fear-inspiring beasts, good mostly as hunting trophies. It would be hard to imagine anyone of that era proclaiming "love" for these big apes. Yet, through her daily observation and physical interaction with the individual gorillas within their families, Dr. Fossey's mind and feelings were transformed. She truly started loving these creatures. Although Dr. Fossey's life and work ended tragically with her murder—not by the gorillas, but probably by poachers—her love for these creatures was transformational. Her book *Gorillas in the Mist,* published in 1985 and later turned into a movie, changed the popular opinion about these animals and mobilized efforts towards their protection. Also, Dr. Fossey herself, by her own account, found her life's fulfillment in her relationship with the mountain gorillas. *Mutual benefit is the fruit of all long-term relationships that have been built upon the first and second principles.*

How many of us in the selling profession have customers or potential customers who we perceive as something like "gorillas in our midst," individuals who elicit in us feelings of apprehension, or perhaps disdain? Maybe we don't do it consciously, but the preconception is there—in the back of our mind. Would our perception of these individuals and customers change if we would take the time to know them, truly get to know them, and then perhaps try to love them even a little? These are tough questions that can only be answered after a deep self-analysis and self-challenge of our perceptions.

Lessons from Thermodynamics

Our understanding of the elusive nature of energy and its applications into useful systems and engines capable of doing work was made possible by the development of the scientific field called "thermodynamics." One of the earliest fruits of this field of study was the development of the steam engine. Without much argument, it could be said the steam engine revolutionized the world. People no longer had to depend on the whims of the wind to travel by sea. With the steam engine, we could produce power when needed, climb mountains pulled by a locomotive, and go upriver in a steamboat. Beautiful in its simplicity, the steam engine was proof that the laws upon which the field of thermodynamics was based were true and useful. Since then, many other engines and machines, including the internal combustion engine, have been developed based on the same laws of thermodynamics.

Why do we bring thermodynamics into a discussion about selling? For two reasons. The first one is to fulfill what was said at the beginning: that this book is built upon enduring principles. The second is rather personal; ever since I was exposed to the laws of thermodynamics in my early twenties, I was fascinated by their usefulness in explaining all the energy-conversion systems that occur in our bodies, our planet, and our universe. And I started thinking how unlikely it would be that something so pervading should have no effect on the way individuals and societies evolve and relate to each other as part of that universe. (The modern findings of fractal theory show that the same patterns repeat themselves in the universe, from the infinitesimal small to the astronomical scale.)

The first law of thermodynamics, also known as the *Law of Conservation of Energy*, has profound implications, and although it can be stated in many ways, one common way is as follows: "The energy in the universe can neither be created nor destroyed, it can only be transferred or transformed." In other words, no matter how hard we may try, neither we humans nor any creature biological or mechanical can create or obliterate energy, only transform it.

Initially, I asked you to look at love as a form of social currency. It is time now that we expand our view of Love—with a capital L—*as a primordial form of energy*. Let's take a closer look at how these same laws apply to Love.

1. Love cannot be created or destroyed

Contrary to popular opinion, you cannot really "make love," at least not in terms of creating it, and there is not a person that has ever succeeded in destroying one picogram of Love. Love is indestructible. There's a confusion between Love, which is indestructible, and *the feeling of love*, which fades away when Love—the energy—is not supplied. An analogy would be for someone to say, "I'm in the dark; someone destroyed my light." Although light was not and cannot be destroyed, the feeling of being in the darkness and not being able to see is valid and real. Yet most of us know that in order to get out of the darkness, we must find a source of light.

Since our effectiveness as social creatures depends heavily on how much Love energy we can give and receive, it is crucially important that we are mindful of habits and activities that cause prohibitive drains on our Love energy level, and conversely pursue habits and activities that restore and enhance it. We started discussing this in the introduction, but chapter 6 will be dedicated to this subject.

2. Love can only be transferred or transformed

As with other forms of energy, it's only by transforming Love that we can produce tangible, measurable effects. In other words, Love that is not put in action is simply *potential energy*. Stephen Covey explains this property of Love by relating the story of a man who came to him after a seminar and complained that there wasn't any love left in his marriage. The man asked Covey for advice on what to do. Covey told him, "Love your wife." The man was perplexed. He replied by saying, "As I mentioned, the feeling is not

there; how do you love when you don't love?"
Covey's answer was in itself a paradigm shift,
"My friend, love is a verb, love—the feeling—is
a fruit of love, the verb. So love her."[8] The profound message is that Love must be put in motion before we obtain its benefit, its fruit. This is
the law of transformation of energy, of transformation of Love.

Now, let's bring this discussion of Love back
to sales. Most salespeople are familiar with the
process of converting the hard features of their
products or services into functions and then into
benefits that their customers can actually see and
appreciate. It is an old adage that customers are
not really interested in buying quarter-inch drill
bits, but rather in making quarter-inch holes.
Early in our sales career, most of us realize that
the *benefit* is really what the customer wants and
buys. So, in our sales pitches with customers we
must carefully select a few features of our product or services and explain how those features
will work for our customer's *benefit*. After some
time and practice, we learn to do this conversion
rather automatically, and for beginning salespeople it is a good skill to acquire. But unless we
understand the underlying principle that makes

this process work, eventually it will sputter and no longer produce the desired results. I'm sure you have been a recipient of a telephone sales pitch and realized immediately how scripted it sounded. We could not see any benefit in the scripted sales proposal.

Remember that an engine is only an instrument of energy conversion. It cannot produce any output of work *without a constant input of energy*. Likewise, the feature-function-benefit process, is an instrument of conversion, nothing more. If we don't realize this, sooner or later we'll find that it stopped producing results like a dead engine out of fuel. The customer does not see the benefit anymore! In essence, we thought we could get something today, tomorrow, and forever by the input of energy from last month. Like the notion of a perpetual motion machine, which violates the first law of thermodynamics, this too will fail to work in the long run.

If we are to succeed in maintaining long-term mutually beneficial relationships with our customers, also called "account management," we must realize that only by the constant input of energy can we truly convert a hard feature into its fruit: *a benefit that is not static*, but is constantly being renovated and that is genuinely cherished and appreciated.

One of the purposes of this book is to differentiate between short- and long-term selling. Most of us realize in our personal lives—say in our marriages—that in order to make a relationship work and be fruitful in the long term, we must pour Love into it, and keep pouring it. It is a journey, not a destination.

Consider this from the customer's point of view: How many people do you think buy a Harley-Davidson motorcycle simply as a mode of transportation?

I had a customer who was the owner of a successful company in Texas. He and a couple of his buddies had made it a ritual to ride their Harleys every year in the fall to Big Bend National Park. After returning from his trip, he was for a while a different man. He literally glowed with energy. He would tell me, "Rudy, when I get on that bike and get going on those empty roads, I feel free. I feel loved. I feel loved by the wind, loved by the sun. I feel the purring of the engine making sort of a symphony with the universe which enfolds me like a mother enfolds his baby." Obviously, he was not referring to a cold, hard machine. He was referring to an instrument of Love.

Now, although the products I was selling at that time did not resemble Harley motorcycles, our company had just launched a new product that was giving excellent results, and for which I eagerly needed early adopters for. I also believed that my customer's company could benefit and increase its revenue from using the product. The experience he had shared with me revealed that this was a person that loved to be outdoors in contact with nature, and he got me thinking of ways I could perhaps match the motorcycle experience.

With approval from my district manager, I engineered and put forth a possible match in the form of a business proposal whereas, in exchange for his company's trial buying and adoption of our new product, I would take him and his two sons—who were also working with him—to a ski resort in Colorado. He accepted my proposal and the ensuing ski trip, combined with the time we all spent together in a cabin next to a warm fire after hitting the slopes, proved to be consequential. I venture to say that at that point our business relationship transitioned to one of friendship as well. He became and early adopter, and by being one of the first companies in the area to start using the new technology, his company differentiated itself from the competition and increased its revenues. With the support of my company, I kept pouring energy into our business relationship in the form of co-op advertisement, technical support, and troubleshooting. On our side, my company benefited not only due to the additional sales revenue, but because my customer became an enthusiastic supporter and promoter of the new technology.

Almost a decade later, after I had left the area and moved to a different sales territory, I ran into one of the sons of my former customer at a business convention. He was now running the business. His company was growing and doing well. And even though many years had passed, he remembered warmly our ski trip and how much it had meant to them, especially to his dad, who was now semiretired. His company was still a very loyal customer of ours.

The marathon salesperson's work is to understand and care about his or her customers enough to know what they want/need, and then challenge himself and his organization to find ways to provide it for them; granted, within the confines of ethical standards and adapting and transforming the products and services the salesperson has to offer. The tactics will be as diverse as the products and services themselves, but the overall strategy—the principle—is the application of Love energy from salesperson to customer, which will return back to the salesperson in the form of higher revenue and other intangibles. Most selling techniques and gimmicks will fail in the long run unless they are in accordance with these natural laws, and unless they provide that energy which is yearned by every human being: Love.

Thus, loving your customers is not a platitude, is not just a nice thing to do, and is not an act of charity. *It is the work, the mission, of all successful marathon salespeople.*

Second Practical Activity

1. Retrieve the customer worksheet you started in chapter 1.
2. Label the fourth column "Customer Needs/ Wants." Focus on each customer at a time. For a moment, stop thinking about the customer as a source of business, and think instead of what he and/or his organization wants or

needs. Try to remember comments or clues the customer may have provided you casually.

3. Write those down on the fourth column, even though you may not have products or services that match their needs/wants exactly.

4. If you come up to a customer and your mind goes blank, just leave the space open for now and go to the next customer. Very often, clues come to us at unexpected times, even in the middle of the night. What's important is that you changed the way you thought about that customer.

5. Label the fifth column "Loving Actions." The next phase may take a few days, even weeks. Thinking outside the box, let your imagination search for assets that you and/or your organization possess that could be used or leveraged to satisfy the customer's needs/wants. This is a first pass—work in progress—we will revisit and complete this column after developing our Personal Talent Inventory in the next chapter.

CHAPTER 3

BECOMING A BLESSING

It is one of the most beautiful com-pensations of this life, that no man can sincerely try to help another without helping himself.
—Ralph Waldo Emerson

In chapter 1, we started the process of changing our perception of our customer base by think-ing of them not only as a source of revenue, but as "blessings," as a source of intangible assets. In this chapter, we will complete the process, this time by changing the perception we have of our-selves. In essence, to start thinking of ourselves as "blessings" as well. In long-term selling, these two facets go hand in hand.

The Third Principle: Serve Those Who You Want to Have as Customers

The Third Principle, "Serve those who you want to have as customers," provides the means by which we keep current costumers satisfied and also the means by which we acquire new customers. It could also be stated as follows:

If you want to increase your opportunities (blessings), you must become an opportunity (blessing) yourself.

If we consider the actions and teachings of great leaders of the past, as we will later in this chapter, we see that they combine humility with confidence. The best sales professionals are not much different. On the one hand, they listen to what their customers say they want and need and are open to their feedback; and, on the other hand, they develop the confidence that their products and services, which are constantly transformed and enhanced by Love energy, are worthy of their customer's time and money.

The Humbling Question

The Third Principle is a humbling one. For arrogance is the enemy of all salespeople. Let's not confuse arrogance with self-confidence. Confidence in yourself and in what you offer is what this book aims to achieve! It's a necessary element of all long-term relationships. *Arrogance*, on the other hand, is a deceptive ego-protecting behavior used mainly to hide a lack: lack of knowledge, lack of Love, lack of empathy, lack of awareness, and so forth. It indicates a disconnected state, disconnection from the blessings and people around you. Arrogance is a killer of long-term relationships. But as with all "lacks," the remedy for arrogance is not to attack it, but to supply that which is lacking. Then arrogance simply disappears as darkness does when light enters a room. Let's explore these concepts in more detail.

Serving others is by nature humbling; and, in order to best serve our current customers and gain *trustworthiness* with those who have chosen not to do business with us *yet*, we must ask humbling questions. One of the most practical sales programs I was privileged to participate early in my sales career was given by a sales consultant named Bill Sharp.[9] In his program, he explained very simple yet powerful techniques for overcoming customer's objections for doing business with us. He emphasized that the first thing to do is to stop talking about your products or services and, instead, ask probing questions with a sincere intent of listening, questions that actually sound like a request for guidance. For instance, "Please help me understand, *for my own benefit*, why you think our price is too high?" Or, "Please help me understand, *in order to allow me to do better in the future*, why you choose not to do business with my company?"

I call these humbling questions because they ask for help from the prospective customer in a very particular way. Arrogant people tend not to ask for help; they just get angry and frustrated. But normally, when someone we know asks for our help and we sense a sincere desire, we tender that help, especially when it's a request for information to make that someone a better person. Between the lines, the question is really saying, "See, I may have had some preconceived notions about the benefit I bring to the table. Obviously, you do not value this benefit as much as I thought you would. So, please tell me how I can increase the value of the benefit to you; help me become a blessing to you."

Once you understand what your customers want/need, you can begin the process of using your assets and those of your company's in creative ways to transform your products and services in a way that your offering somehow matches their expectations. Again, remember that this is a labor of Love.

The One Action That Speaks a Thousand Words

Customers or prospective customers do not automatically see us as "blessings." Again, *blessings* are opportunities that when recognized and acted upon bring some form of prosperity—material, emotional, mental, or spiritual. Let's not confine prosperity only to the material realm. A good teacher is certainly a blessing by increasing the intellectual, emotional, and spiritual prosperity of his or her students without necessarily increasing their bank accounts. In fact, the mark of all good salespeople is that their customers see them not just as sellers of goods and services but as resources, teachers, trainers—people to go to for reliable information, capable of even respectfully challenging a customer's blind spots.

Becoming a "blessing" is a process. It begins with an actual paradigm shift that occurs in the minds of customers or prospective customers that causes them to see the salesperson in a different light. In order for this paradigm shift to occur, the salesperson and customer must start with a clean slate. In other words, they must clear away all preconceived notions of what salespeople are.

Thousands of years ago, enlightened spiritual masters discovered that one single action produced a fundamental change in the hearts of people—a paradigm shift. It was washing the feet of those with who they wanted to establish a long-term relationship. Washing the feet was a powerful action that spoke a thousand words. It meant that a true master is one who's willing to serve.[10] How Ironic! With the simple act of washing the feet, arrogance left the relationship so that mutual trust and bonding could take place. In many cultures, washing the feet became a symbol of forgiveness; forgiveness in the sense of starting anew.

Letting go of the past is a necessary step in the process of establishing long-term relationships (a subject that will be covered in more detail in the next chapters). As salespeople, one of the greatest challenges we face is to find that one action—for it must be an action—which in the eyes of prospective customers is the equivalent of washing their feet, the one action that changes their thinking about us and allows them to see us in a different light. You will read an example of this concept in Chapter 5 of this book.

The Third Principle should not be interpreted as a directive for salespeople to become subservient. It by no means encourages you to become the subject of abuse or to give in to dishonest advances by those who you seek to do business with. These are all lose-win situations and, therefore, not sustainable. Integral to the Third Principle is the recognition that we all possess unique talents and that the way to increase our prosperity (i.e., our customer base) is to share those talents in ways that are also unique. (You will read more on that concept below.) One of the greatest social revolutions of modern times was the advancement of the concept that kings, governments, and laws are put in place to *serve the people*, not the other way around. Paradoxically, the status of kings and governors who truly served their people grew rather than diminished. This paradox is demonstrated amply in nature. Does the status of the sun diminish because it shines on earth? Do we think less of an apple tree because it shares its fruit with us? On the contrary, we tend to the apple tree and help spread its seeds. The Third Principle, then, is a directive to share our unique talents in order to create a benefit for those who we seek to have as customers and increase our prosperity—a win-win situation.

The Treasure

Few individuals know at an early age what their gifts are. Those that do, such as Wolfgang Amadeus Mozart and Isaac Newton, are known as "child prodigies," and perhaps you know of or have encountered others in your life. They are the exception. The rest of us go through a long part of our lives without really knowing what our unique talents are. Therefore, we don't share them. It's not that we don't want to share but that we think we're "poor." Sometimes it takes a special event or even a series of misfortunes to make us realize what our talents are. Einstein considered himself a failure, a talentless individual, for a major part of his life. However, he certainly made it up in the latter part of his life. For most of us, the discovery and development of our talents involves a long journey. Often, we come to realize the unique talents we possess only with the help from others.

Many years ago, I came across a children's book I used to read to my daughters when they were little. I still keep a copy even though my daughters are all grown up. *The Treasure*, written by Uri Shulevitz, illustrates this elusive process of discovery in a brief and most impactful way.

The story is about a man who was very poor. He kept having recurrent dreams in which a voice told him to go to the capital city and search for a treasure hidden under a bridge located by the royal palace. He dismissed the dreams initially, but when they kept occurring, he decided to take the long journey from his village to the capital city. Along the way, he got help from strangers who gave him rides for parts of his journey, but mostly he walked alone.

When he finally arrived at the capital city and went to the bridge of his dreams, he found that it was constantly guarded. Fearful, he didn't dare search for the treasure, but kept coming to the bridge every day and just wandered around, not knowing what do to. One day, the captain of the guards approached him and asked him for the reason of his constant presence. He humbly told the captain about his dream. In response, the captain laughingly pitied him for coming such a long way for a dream and told him that he too had a dream once where he found a treasure under the stove in a house that belonged to a person named "Isaac." He silently bowed to the captain, for Isaac was his name. He then took the long journey back to his town.

When he finally arrived, he went to his house and dug under his stove where he did find the treasure. Gratefully, he sent the captain a jewel and built a chapel where one could read the following inscription: "Sometimes one must travel far to discover what is near."[11]

I was lucky to learn such a timeless lesson from a children's book. The truth is that there is no person on earth who is born without a "treasure." But, like in the story, it may be hidden. It may be hidden very near us—*perhaps within us.* Sometimes we must travel far to discover what was always within our reach. Very often it is through interaction with other people that we discover our treasure. That is the purpose of the next exercise, which is discovering your Personal Talent Inventory (PTI).

The Personal Talent Inventory – Group Exercise

A team of coworkers, associates, or even close friends can carry out this mutually beneficial group exercise. The group must consist of people who know each other well and are willing to offer one another helpful insights. In its most basic format, a facilitator is chosen from the group who writes the names of each participant on individual index cards and distributes the cards to all participants. Each participant receives as many cards as there are participants in the group minus one—his own. Then, each participant is given the following instructions:

1. Think thoroughly about the person whose name is written on the card and write down two or three unique talents he or she possesses that immediately pop into your mind.
2. Now, dig a little deeper. What talent do you think this person has which he or she *may not realize?* Put in other terms, what talent could this person *easily develop from what he already has* that could become a real strength? This

could take the form of, "You are gifted at this. Have you thought about using it for that?" It requires that each person becomes somewhat of a coach to the others. Remember, good coaches see potential.

3. Lastly, as you go through the exercise, remember that others will also be doing the same for you. The Golden Rule must be applied!

4. Do this for each person you have received cards for.

The completed cards are sent back to the facilitator who will compile them and distribute or send to their owners. Alternatively, this whole process can be done, via email as long as the rules above are followed and each participant receives honest feedback on his or her unique talents from the rest of the group.

Taking Possession

When you receive the cards or emails written by you peers, take a good look at the talents others see in you. But know that the list compiled by your peers *is not your real treasure.* These are only hints and directions to your real treasure, the equivalent of the captain's comments in the story. You are the only one who can dig out your own treasure. *For unless you take possession of the talents listed on your PTI, they are not yours!* You will only see them as a dream. Perhaps you may laugh at some of them. You will be reluctant to use them, which is the same as not having them. Search for patterns; are there talents that are mentioned more than once? More than twice? Those are like recurrent dreams you can no longer ignore.

After some introspection, and using the PTI as your base, write down *in your own words*, five talents you believe you have and two that you could develop. More if you wish. Review your list often and expand. These will become your real treasure.

The talents you take possession of and internalize are essentially the only things, besides your product or service, you can bring to the table to become a true blessing for your customers and those who you want as customers. As you become comfortable with your talents and use them to serve and create unique benefits, you will gain genuine self-confidence, which in turn will dispel arrogance, the enemy of all salespeople.

The Gender Factor

This chapter would not be complete without an honest and practical discussion about the variables that arise in the field of sales and customer relationships as a result of gender, and how it may affect our application and practice of the Third Principle.

We need to start by restating unequivocally that although the Third Principle is a humbling one, it by no means constitutes a directive to surrender your dignity as a person in exchange for business or to expect anyone else to do so. Any business or benefit obtained in this way is short-lived and unsustainable. Let's remember that the means to serve your customers and those who you want as customers is to share your talents without sacrificing your capacity. That is the overriding strategy. Talents are regenerative. A virtuoso violinist that performs and shares her music at a concert hall does not lose her capacity to deliver another beautiful performance at a later date and then at another. In fact, she may even get better after each performance. But what happens if in the course of securing a new performance, someone or something causes her to become so despondent that she loses the joy of performing? In this case, her production capacity has been seriously impaired.

It is a reality that women face certain challenges in the field of sales that most men do not. For this segment, I surveyed a few former female colleagues who had successful careers in sales for their insights. I also have four daughters, all college graduates, who are now working in their chosen fields. It is through all their collective experience and conversations that I learned and continue to learn how certain events that men consider inconsequential, like going to a bar with customers or coworkers for a drink or two, can become career-limiting events for women. Yet, a lot of buying decisions don't happen at formal meetings but at golf courses or in the course of having a meal or a few drinks at those bars. Therefore, avoiding social outings with customers altogether would not be an advantageous solution for women.

Many books have recently been published by women from various industries about sexual harassment in the workplace, and I expect many more will be added to the toolbox to help us all better understand these issues: for men, to gain empathy about the unique challenges women face in the workforce and to become more enlightened men; for women, to help them prepare to handle sexual harassment situations, when to seek assistance, or report to the proper authorities if necessary. This book's offerings on this subject are limited and practical in nature, but hopefully they will provide a primer for those still young and new in the field of sales.

Summarized below are some pointers and tactical advice for women (and men) compiled from comments and experiences offered by veteran female salespeople:

1. If you are a young female salesperson coming into a new sales territory, talk to other women who have been in the field for some time, even if they are in different territories. They will offer you invaluable information about the men who misuse their position of power over unsuspecting female vendors in your particular industry.

2. Whether male or female, whenever you are at a bar having drinks with customers, be mindful of the effects of alcohol. After one alcoholic drink or two, opt for nonalcoholic drinks or drink a glass of water between each alcoholic beverage. That way you are happy to have a drink, but don't have your judgment impaired.

3. At the beginning of a relationship with a prospective customer of the opposite sex who happens to be married, invite both husband and wife, especially if dinner is what is planned for entertainment.

4. Once the relationship with the customer has progressed and has well-established boundaries, opt for lunches rather than dinners for one-on-one entertainment. Lunches are usually quicker and more casual.

5. Know and become an expert on what you are selling and the benefits you bring to the customer. This will give you self-confidence and command respect without sounding arrogant.

6. Do not allow yourself to be intimidated under any circumstances. You are not asking for charity. If you believe and follow the principles explained in this book, you should know that, above all, you are a blessing and you bring unique talents that no one else has.

7. If you are ever in a situation where you become a victim of sexual harassment, be sure to contact your HR department or another trusted expert to help you figure out the next steps to protect yourself and others.

8. During your sales career, you will invariably have to deal with some customers who get

frustrated, sometimes downright angry, especially when they feel their legitimate expectations are not being met. Some will call you up and express their frustrations, which is good, because then you can make amendments or calibrate your offerings better. In fact, they are doing you a favor. This is preferable to them moving their business to your competition without telling you anything. Most customers will not stay angry for long if they feel you are truly listening to their concerns with empathy and with the intention of making things better. Very often, you will gain more respect and strengthen the relationship after you have managed to resolve their issues.

9. However, it is also possible that some customers may feel entitled to express their frustration by subjecting you to verbal abuse. If or when this happens, it is absolutely critical that you acknowledge their anger but don't allow the conversation to go any further. When things have cooled down, you should provide reassurance that the issues will be addressed but let them know that their words have crossed a line and have hurt you, and you will not allow that to happen again. Following

is an account of how a female sales colleague
handled a situation of this nature:

> I was on vacation, driving with my
> two daughters in the car, when my
> phone started ringing. I realized
> the call was from one of my larg-
> est customers, so I decided to take
> the call. I had to put him on the
> speakerphone   [company-policy
> mandated   hands-free   operation
> of a phone while driving]. But he
> proceeded to curse and to get into
> a personal attack. After my initial
> shock, I immediately said to him,
> "I am hanging up now. I'm on va-
> cation and have my two girls in the
> car. I will get back to you later."
> The following day, I went to see
> the customer and said something
> like, "I was on vacation with my
> two daughters yesterday. I took
> the call only because I saw it was
> from you. I'm here to help resolve
> the issue. I'm not your adversary,
> but don't ever treat me like you
> did yesterday. You wouldn't talk

> to your daughters or your wife
> like that, would you? Why would
> you treat me so differently?" He
> apologized and after many years
> he still remains a good customer.

This account has so many teaching elements that it's worth analyzing it and making a few comments along the way.

First, the customer was acknowledged and assured that he would be heard at a later time, but he could not continue the abusive behavior.

After a short cooldown period, and to reinforce the urgency of the situation, the salesperson went to see the customer personally.

The ensuing conversation had four important elements, all flowing rapidly but working effectively in combination:

1. She reaffirmed how important the customer was to her by reminding him that she had taken the call the previous day even though she was on vacation only because she saw the call was from him.

2. She reassured the customer that she was there not as an adversary, but to serve as his advocate. This is crucial, notice the application of

the Third Principle—*to serve*. In situations like this, the customer is seeking reassurance that we've got his back. In contrast, notice how you felt last time you called the "customer service" department of a corporation with a complaint, and after many frustrating auto-mated messages, you finally got connected to a real person only to realize that the person was not your advocate at all, that you were barking up the wrong tree?

3. She expressed clearly and unambiguously how the customer's words and behavior had crossed the line, especially in her situation as a mom with her young children getting ex-posed to those words. She reminded the cus-tomer that she was also a person, like his own family, and she asked to be treated with the same respect.

4. Finally, she asked the customer point-blank not to ever treat her with such disrespect again.

In their bestselling book *The One Minute Sales Person*[12], the authors reveal a few insightful re-minders that successful sales people practice to become better. I'd like to bring out a couple of those reminders that I found were at work in the previous account to wrap up our discussion of the Third Principle:

"Behind every sale is a person." This works both ways. Obviously, we must never forget that customers are people, not just numbers, but sometimes customers need to be reminded that we, salespeople, are also persons, not just entities from a large corporation devoid of feelings or self-respect.

"Whenever I see that my sales behavior is unacceptable to me, I take a minute to reprimand my behavior and to praise myself." Again, this can be used both for ourselves and for our customers. Differentiating the behavior from the actual person is a great insight. Behaviors can be changed and improved, both our behavior and the customer's. Although the idea of reprimanding a customer may sound abhorrent, it can be done effectively. Notice the effective combination of praise (acknowledgement, validation, love) and reprimand (a firm request that a hurtful and unacceptable behavior be not repeated).

But what if a particular customer is in the habit of crossing the line with you, or whose business practices are incompatible? As a marathon salesperson, chances are that you will encounter these situations sooner or later. Part of account management is to perform "selective pruning" of your customer base periodically. This will be discussed on the next chapter, and in greater detail, on the final chapter of this book.

In summary, whether you are a woman or a man, and if you are with me this far, you should realize now that you possess many real talents that can be brought to the table for the benefit of your current customers and for the acquisition of new ones. This knowledge is powerful because it also acts as a shield that protects you from being demeaned. As such, *serving those who you want as customers* is done from a position of strength, without arrogance. And that is the equivalent of *becoming a blessing.*

Third Practical Activity

At this time, you can retrieve your customer spreadsheet. Now, using your newly discovered and appropriated talents, take a second pass at brainstorming ways to enhance your offering to each of your current customers and write those down in the fifth column (Loving Actions). You may also add the names of prospective customers to your list and complete this activity with them in mind.

CHAPTER 4

PLANTING AND HARVESTING

Nature herself does not distinguish between what seed it receives. It grows whatever seed is planted; this is the way life works. Be mindful of the seeds you plant today, as they will become the crop you harvest.
—Mary Morrissey

The Fourth Principle is truly universal. It applies to any life path, but especially to long-term endeavors. It contains two directives designed to work together to ensure sustainability in your marathon sales journey.

The Fourth Principle: Plant Good Seeds and Balance Your Planting and Harvesting

The first directive of this principle "Plant good seeds" has been expressed in many ways from East to West. "A man reaps what he sows," is found in biblical scriptures, and the law of karma states that every action has a consequence either immediate or delayed.

Unless you are a salesperson coming into a brand-new territory, a large part of the business you are harvesting today was probably planted years ago, either by you or by someone before you. If the seeds planted were good, in all likelihood you are the beneficiary of a good business harvest. But it is also possible that your predecessors may have sowed some bad seed and you are now the recipient of a territory riddled with thorns and unproductive customer relationships. Some of these relationships can be restored, and the Second and Third Principles we discussed can be used to do so. However, some thorny relationships will never be able to bear good fruit. They have either been alienated beyond repair or may be "losing propositions." They must be selectively pruned. We will discuss this subject more extensively in chapter 6.

My friend and veteran salesman Sid Funk used to make wine as one of his hobbies and was very knowledgeable about the science and art of growing healthy grapes. He told an elegant metaphor to illustrate the balancing between planting, pruning and harvesting. He called it "Lessons from a Vineyard."

> The most productive grape vines are more than fifty years old. A huge amount of care has been invested into these vines to get the very best grapes. But, like a smart vineyard master, in business we can't just rely on our "old vines" and we must constantly plant new cuttings to continue to grow our business. An excellent example of this would be working through the turnover in a large company. Although you used to have an excellent relationship with the branch manager, that doesn't mean a thing to the new person on the other side of the desk. You must constantly plant new seeds and

nurture the saplings so that you always have something to harvest.

Just as some of the best wines are a mélange of grapes from both old and new vines, the best, most sustainable business results from a combination of old and new business relationships. You must attend to the different stages of maturation of your customer relationships to continue to grow your business.[13]

A consequence of applying the principle's first directive is a realization that we are all links in a chain that either benefits or suffers from the legacy of our own planting and/or that of our predecessors. For this reason, the Fourth Principle also obliges us to leave a good legacy to those who will follow us. This last directive is also supported by the Golden Rule.

Keeping the Balance

Realistically, businesses in general and salespeople in particular face constant pressure to maximize the harvesting with minimum planting, or to harvest without planting altogether, especially in so-called "bad times." Indeed, it's very tempting to go for the "quick sale," for maximizing profits and slashing costs to the bone. This provides instant gratification and results. However, the lack of balance violates natural laws and, therefore, is not an effective or sustainable practice. It invariably leads to the degradation, alienation, and even collapse of those assets or relationships responsible for producing revenue. Many metaphors have been written to illustrate this point, but I believe the most vivid and memorable is Stephen Covey's use of Aesop's timeless fable "The Goose That Laid the Golden Eggs."[14]

> There was once a countryman who possessed the most wonderful goose you can imagine, for every day when he visited the nest, the goose had laid a beautiful, glittering, golden egg.
>
> The countryman took the eggs to market and soon began to get rich. But it was not long before he grew impatient with the goose because she gave him only a single golden

egg a day. He was not getting rich fast enough.

Then one day, after he had finished counting his money, the idea came to him that he could get all the golden eggs at once by killing the goose and cutting it open. But when the deed was done, not a single golden egg did he find, and his precious goose was dead.

Although not as drastic as killing the goose outright, I have seen in my sales career other tactics being employed which are the equivalent to forcing the goose to lay more and more eggs quickly, which eventually sickens the goose or kills it. For instance, it's possible to "sell through intimidation," and in fact there are many advocates of this practice in the business world. It can produce fast results from unsuspecting first-time buyers; therefore, it becomes almost an addictive practice. From the sellers' perspective "everything is great." But, sooner or later, customers realize individually and collectively that "something is wrong with this business/industry." If you ever bought a car from an old-school dealership, you know how emotionally draining the whole process was. Even when you ended buying a decent car, you were pressured by the salesperson to buy unnecessary or superfluous fees, add-ons, and/or services solely designed to squeeze every customer for maximum profit. A feeling of alienation ensued. Your view of the dealership's trustworthiness suffered significantly, resulting in a very low desire to do business with them in the future. During the last decade, new car dealerships started emerging with a different paradigm: to make the process less *intimidating* and more transparent and buyer-friendly, even rewarding. They realized that the old process was unsustainable in the long run.

To summarize, the Fourth Principle builds upon the previous ones to ensure that a sustainable flow of prosperity—blessings—is established and kept going between salespeople and customers. It directs us to keep a healthy balance between the revenue extracted from the customers and the investment necessary to keep those customers satisfied. In business and nature, this flow is symbolized and governed by the laws of planting and harvesting.

Fourth Practical Activity

A good exercise based on this principle is to examine each of your customers. Not just the ones that are producing good fruit, but also the ones that are not. On the sixth column of your spreadsheet, make a note about the positive and negative impacts that you or your predecessor may have had with each customer. Then write down potential activities that will ensure long-term continuity with each of the customers you are engaged. Perhaps establishing new contacts within some of the organizations experiencing growth or personnel turnover or establishing loyalty programs with some of your long-term customers.

A Review Before the Fifth Principle

At this point it will be useful to summarize the material we have discussed so far, which will serve as the foundation for the next principle.

The First Principle establishes that the starting point on the road to prosperity in the field of sales and in every walk of life is to become aware of our blessings and quantify them. It also establishes that we don't live in a vacuum, and that at all times, we are surrounded by blessings that come in the shape of opportunities. But in order to take advantage of these opportunities, we must tune our mind so we can perceive what were blurred images before, the development of a Grateful Mind.

The Second Principle establishes the laws of energy and Love, and that it is impossible to get something for nothing. It is only through the conversion of Love energy that we produce genuine, sustainable benefits for our customers.

The Third Principle builds upon the previous two and is the way to keep our current customers satisfied and to acquire new customers. It directs us to discover our innate talents—treasure—to take possession of those talents and utilize them in unique ways to customize and enhance our offerings, thus becoming a blessing to our customers.

The Fourth Principle further establishes two fundamental concepts. First, we must maintain a balance of planting and harvesting and resist the urge to harvest prematurely, "killing the goose that lays the golden eggs." Second, we are all links in a chain. If you are obtaining fruits today, it is because someone before you planted and/or poured energy into that which you may be harvesting today. The care of a vineyard is a vivid analogy in the sense that in order to succeed in the long run, we must all be planters, pruners, and harvesters.

CHAPTER 5

THE ELEMENTS OF COMPETITION

Competition whose motive is merely to compete, to drive some other fellow out, never carries very far. The competitor to be feared is one who never bothers about you at all, but goes on making his own business better all the time. Businesses that grow by development and improvement do not die. But when a business ceases to be creative, when it believes it has reached perfection and needs to do nothing but produce

—no improvement, no development—it is done.

—Henry Ford

Most of the concepts we discussed so far in this book about establishing long-term sales practices and relationships dealt with us and our customers or prospective customers—basically a two-way relationship. Competition brings a new dimension to any sales relationship. In reality, competition is a continuously evolving two-way process. Competition affects us; in response we affect the field in which we compete; this changes the field of competition further, which then affects us in different ways than before. This cycle repeats itself. The long-term outcome of this repetitive cycle is a more efficient system. A special form of competition, *cooperative competition*, has been a driving force of evolution. We will focus on this form of competition at the end of this chapter, but first, let's state the Fifth Principle.

The Fifth Principle: Understand and Value
Your Competition

The Fifth Principle, "Understand and value your competition," might cause some head scratching. The importance of understanding competition is rather obvious, but you may ask why in the world you should "value" your competition. We'll provide answers to that question throughout this chapter, but first let's focus on understanding the anatomy of competition.

In any field of endeavor, we can find elements that are within our realm of influence, and that we can master or even use for our benefit. By doing so, our competitive edge becomes sharper automatically. Anyone who has played golf soon realizes that factors other than competing players may have a larger impact on one's game. The wind, the clubs, the golf course, and one's own limitations—or "lacks." Can we truly "win" against the wind? No, but certainly we can try to understand and collaborate with the wind. And anyone who runs a marathon knows about *heartbreak hills*—those extremely challenging segments of the run that you must master by understanding your own physiology and taking care of your own hydration, energy as well as oxygen requirements and consumption, even your own state of mind.

In the field of sales, as you will see, the tools needed to deal effectively with some of the components of competition have already been discussed in previous chapters. Let's review:

There are three major components of competition a salesperson faces:

1. Ignorance, which comes from a lack of knowledge and customer intimacy.
2. Mistrust, which comes from a lack of Love.
3. Market competitors.

Any salesperson who sees market competitors as the only variable is missing two thirds of the equation. Additionally, notice that two of the major competing components a salesperson faces are "lacks." The way to overcome them is to supply what is lacking.

Ignorance: The First Greatest Competitor

Ignorance in sales is basically lack of product and customer knowledge and intimacy. Every salesperson coming into a new territory must overcome ignorance on his or her part by learning everything possible about the product itself and the customer base. The First Principle, "Count your blessings," is the starting point of the process of learning about your customer base. But we must also help our customers and prospective customers to overcome their ignorance about us, about what we sell, and about what we can do. Sales and marketing campaigns will help us do this, but in the end, all the marketing campaigns in the world cannot develop customer intimacy. This can only be accomplished by the salesperson's application of all the principles we have discussed so far.

Mistrust: The Second Greatest Competitor

Similarly, *mistrust* is basically lack of Love. Mistrust is the default state of any relationship until Love is introduced. Mistrust is a form of fear: fear of being cheated, fear of being taken advantage of, fear of not getting a good deal (lose–win). Some form of unconscious fear is always present at the start of any new relationship. A long-term selling relationship, like a marriage, requires the continuous input of energy or the relationship falls back into its default state. There is no such thing as "love 'em and leave 'em" in long-term selling relationships. The Second Principle,

"Love your customers," is critically important to overcome this competitor, followed by the Third Principle, "Serve those who you want to have as customers."

A salesperson who is always conscious of these two competitors, ignorance and mistrust, and works diligently to master them is in a much stronger position to deal effectively with the third, market competitors.

Market Competitors

A good assessment of a sales territory would not be complete without a detailed picture of all the market entities with which we are competing, what our relative position is in this market, and what our vulnerabilities are. A very practical tool to help us bring this detailed picture into focus is called a *SWOT Analysis*, an exercise designed to examine our industry, market, and territory and realistically assess its Strengths, Weaknesses, Opportunities, and Threats (SWOT). In some cases, this analysis leads to questioning our own business model and whether it is prone to disruption by competitors and especially by technological or environmental changes. Let's take a look at some classic examples to illustrate how this analysis works.

In the nineteenth century, the horse and buggy industry flourished as a mode of transportation throughout Europe, Canada, and the United States.[15] In the United States alone, there were thousands of companies that manufactured carriages and many more that repaired and serviced them. There were luxury buggies that the upper class bought, as well as horse-drawn carriages that ran on rails used in public transportation. Other businesses came along that manufactured and sold parts for these buggies and carriages.

Now, imagine for a moment that you are working in this industry early in the twentieth century, right before the advent of Ford's Model T. In the next twenty years, the great majority of buggy and carriage manufacturers would go out of business with thousands of people losing their jobs, salesmen included. Yet, in the midst of this disruption and change, some companies managed to survive and even thrive. At first glance, the companies that were able to transition successfully to the "horseless carriage" or automotive age, were the ones whose products or services could easily be adapted to requirements of the new technology. For example, The Timken

Company, which originally made roller bearings for wheels of horse buggies and carriages, started making roller bearings for automobiles. At the time of this writing, Timken was still doing well, providing components for wind turbines and power transmission systems. "Anything that turns" provides a potential market for Timken and, over the ages, it has adapted its business model to provide offerings to new emerging technologies. Likewise, other companies that made or sold parts for carriages, especially metal parts, were able to adapt their offerings to the automotive industry, and many are still in business today. These companies saw the *threats* to the marketplace and discovered the *opportunities* for them within the new landscape.

As I was conducting the final editing of this book, the COVID-19 pandemic struck. The disruption caused to people and businesses by this event is unfathomable and will be felt for many years to come. Millions of businesses have closed globally and, undoubtedly, many more will close permanently. But others are reinventing themselves and their business models. Below is an account written by Dawson Church, Ph.D., that illustrates this point.

During the early days of the COVID-19 pandemic, the streets of my northern California town were almost empty. On a walk, I passed a favorite local hangout, Murphy's pub. A handwritten cardboard sign caught my eye:

"Closed Permanently. We don't see light at the end of this tunnel. Thanks for a great 31 years."

Behind the door was the dark and empty dining room. I felt sad as I walk down the block, passing many other shops, all shuttered.

That same week, my wife Christine and I were tired of our own cooking after weeks of "sheltering in place," so we called Betty's BBQ. Thirty minutes later, we picked up our order. It was in a bag on a table in front of the dining room doors. Betty herself stood behind the table.

"How is your place doing?" I asked.

"Great!" she replied. "I've been thinking about starting a take-out business for years, and social distancing gave me just the shove I needed." I then asked her about the dining room staff.

"We're so busy that I moved them all into the kitchen to work on food preparation," she explained.

I marveled as I drove away with my BBQ order. When confronted with the same problem—regulations that shut down their dining rooms, the loss of their source of income—the two restaurant owners acted in opposite ways. One shut down, the other invented a new business.[16]

A closer look into the practices of companies that are able not only to survive but to benefit from technological or environmental changes reveal some common threads. First, they look at what they have and what they do well; they "count their blessings," and then they figure out how to become an opportunity, a blessing, to current and prospective customers. The First Principle ("Count your blessings") and the Third Principle ("Serve those who you want to have as customers") in action! In other words, applying the principles in this book will help you immensely as you undertake your SWOT analysis.

If it's that simple, why do most businesses collapse in times of technological or environmental disruptions? One of the most formidable roadblocks that prevents corporations from applying these principles is a deeply entrenched loyalty to "The Way We Do Business" (TWWDB). When we've been in a particular business for a long time, we have considerable amount of emotion, time, capital, and other things invested in TWWDB. With time, we become staunch defenders neither of the business itself nor the customers, but of TWWDB. Again, I turn to Stephen Covey for an elegant metaphor to illustrate this point.

Covey tells the story of a team of people who are cutting a path through a jungle with machetes. The team is well organized and consists not only of strong, capable machete-wielders, but also behind them, there is a team of managers and support personnel that sharpen the machetes, hold muscle development programs, write policy manuals, and set up working schedules and compensation programs for the machete workers. Then one of the men who Covey calls "the leader" climbs the tallest tree and after surveying the landscape yells, "Wrong jungle!" From below, the various managers of the team respond, "Shut up! We're making progress."[17] The managers are so invested in their familiar jungle and in the progress they have made in it, that they will sternly resist moving to another, until they run into a swamp, and even then, they may rationalize that it is only a puddle.

Going back to the horse-drawn vehicle industry, if you were the owner or salesperson of a company that sold horse buggies, and a few of your loyal customers started telling you that they were no longer interested in buying your product, but were contemplating buying an automobile instead, what would you have done? Would you have, (A) laughed at these customers and dismissed the idea of a horseless carriage as impractical, costly, and absurd; (B) became internally angry with these customers and focused on how ungrateful they were after the easy financing, free repairs, and everything you had provided to them over the years; or, (C) listened to them carefully and asked them to *please explain to you, for your own benefit, why they thought your product and services no longer satisfied their needs* (the humbling question in chapter 3)?

When Ford's Model T, the "Tin Lizzie" as it was called, made its debut in 1908, I venture to say there must have been an overwhelming number of salespeople and managers who responded as in A or B above. However, a few "leaders" in the carriage industry, especially the ones who had direct contact with customers, asked their customers questions similar to C above, and realized that a powerful competitor was entering the market and that their business was running into a swamp.

It is beyond the scope of this book to discuss the fault lines of the decision-making process made by executives and board of directors of large corporations that eventually lead them to bankruptcy or obsolescence. However, I maintain that it is the responsibility of good salespeople to convey to owners or to upper management within their realm of influence, the legitimate concerns of customers as well as potential threats posed by competitors that could disrupt their relationships. Upper management may ignore your warnings or even tell you to "shut up," but at least you have done your part. The salesperson's loyalty is, and ultimately must be, to the customer, not to the product or service that's being sold or to "The Way We Do Business."

That may sound like anathema, but history has proven repeatedly that even the most popular products and services fade away and become obsolete. Think about horse buggies, film cameras, encyclopedias, Blockbuster video stores, public pay phones, and many more. *Yet, customers live on.*

When doing the SWOT analysis, if we start with the question, "How can we continue to be a blessing to our customers," rather than, "How can we sell them more products," we may see opportunities we had not seen before. We may find that some of our perceived "strengths" are no longer valid and are beginning to crumble. But most important, we may find out that within the realm of knowledge and expertise of our own person, our peers, our division, and our company, there is a capacity to modify and enhance our offerings to better suit the needs of our customers and to continue to be a blessing to them. I hope to further illustrate these concepts by the following account of my own experience.

A SWOT Analysis Case Study

One year after graduating from college with a Bachelor of Science degree, I accepted a job with The Dow Chemical Company, working in a lab as a biochemist.

Eight years went by very fast while working and taking graduate courses at night towards an MBA degree—a benefit Dow offered that reimbursed me for the expenses of taking the courses. I didn't realize then how useful and consequential taking these courses were going to be for my career. One day, I learned through my supervisor about opportunities that were opening up in sales and marketing for employees with technical backgrounds in the company's agricultural division. My supervisor thought that I had the right mix of skills to make me a good candidate and encouraged me to apply. Little did I know then that I would be embarking on a career in sales and marketing that spawned twenty-seven years.

My first job in this new field was as a sales specialist in southeast Florida. One of the products

I was in charge of selling was a specialty gas fumigant used for the control of *drywood termites* (a type of termite that lives entirely inside the wood of a structure and needs no contact with the soil) and other wood-infesting insects in homes and structures. A gas fumigant, because of its expanding properties, is uniquely effective in reaching every nook and cranny of a structure where termites may be living and where liquids or aerosols cannot possibly reach. But it also requires specially trained individuals to apply it, keep it under confinement for the period of time necessary to do its job, and perform the aeration with specialized equipment so that the structure can be made safe for reoccupation. In granting registration for the product, one of the requirements of the Environmental Protection Agency (EPA) was that it could only be sold to and used by certified applicators or people under their direct supervision. To this date, structural fumigation is a very specialized facet of pest control that must be done by professionals.

At the time I came to Florida as a sales specialist, there was another gas fumigant competing with ours. The competing product was effective in controlling drywood termites and cost less than ours. Those were a couple of hard facts

I had to accept. Naturally, because it worked well and was less expensive, most fumigation companies were using the competing product almost exclusively, but there were a few companies that were using both products, theirs and ours. Voila! I quickly determined that one of my first priorities in doing the SWOT analysis of my territory had to be to find out why a company would possibly use our product when it costs more. Well, I learned that the physical properties of both fumigants were not the same. There was, for instance, a significant difference in the *boiling points* (i.e., the temperature at which a liquid turns into a gas) of both fumigants. This affected the requirements needed to introduce each fumigant into the structure. The competing product required the use of a heat exchanger, an extra piece of equipment to warm the fumigant. Ours did not. The same physical property also affected the speed at which each fumigant dissipated from the structure once the fumigation was completed. Our product dissipated, or *desorbed*, much faster; this meant that the fumigation process took less time to complete, and therefore, in a lot of cases, where time was of essence, the savings in time compensated for the extra cost of our product.

But that was not all. I also learned that due to a difference in another physical property, the competing product had a propensity to react with carpet padding, some rubber products, and other sulfur-containing items commonly found in homes. If a reaction occurred, a bad odor similar to rotten eggs would result. Although the odor itself was not toxic, it did not sit well with homeowners who returned to their homes after the fumigation. The remedy of replacing carpet padding and other items was not only disruptive to the homeowner but also costly to the fumigator. For this reason, some fumigators had instituted a policy that if a house had carpeting, it could not be fumigated with the competing product. But even if a house didn't have carpet, there was always a risk that some overlooked household item would react and cause problems and extra costs.

It was at this time that I realized that the fact that our product was more expensive was not an insurmountable barrier to its greater acceptance and sales. I began to see that my greatest competitor was not the other product, but *ignorance* (the first of the three main components of competition for salespeople).

First, I needed to overcome ignorance on my part by learning everything I possibly could not only about fumigants and their physical properties, but also about their history, the fumigation process, the equipment, the innovations and innovators, and even the regulations. Second, I needed to overcome ignorance on the part of prospective fumigator customers about myself and about how the advantages of using our product compensated more than enough for its extra price.

To achieve these goals, I embedded myself temporarily in the fumigation crew of one of our customers who graciously assigned me to one of their fumigation "ground crews." In the process, I learned the terminology and the importance of ground preparation to achieve optimal fumigation. I became aware and appreciative of the strength and hard physical work that was required to completely wrap a building in impermeable heavy-duty tarps from the roof to the ground. It was like gift-wrapping a house. I developed calluses on my knuckles, which in the fumigation industry is the clear, unmistakable proof that you have worked with fumigation tarps.

But most important, the action of becoming a fumigation worker gave me credibility in the eyes of fumigators. Word went around. I was no longer just the "new guy from Dow." In the eyes of the customer who allowed me to be his worker, this was the one action that was the equivalent of "washing his feet," discussed in chapter 3. Moreover, perhaps just as important, even though I did not realize it at that time, it confirmed what I'd been hearing from colleagues and others in the industry: that there was a great need for manufacturers' support in the industry that was not yet fully met. It also started a process in my mind to search for ways to improve the way training in fumigation was provided in general.

The evolution of these two concepts, *superior support* and *better training*, became almost an obsession and the cornerstone of our offering along with the fumigant. It called for our moving to a proverbial "different jungle," one where Dow not only manufactured and sold the product but took an increasingly active role in how well it was used. These various support activities came under the umbrella name of *Product Stewardship*. The move proved to be right and crucial, as new regulations were coming into effect, and the pest control industry in general and the fumigation industry in particular were coming under greater scrutiny and pressure to apply pesticides safely.

Fortunately, Dow's Agricultural Division managers were not only supportive but encouraging of this endeavor. Most important, management made resources available in the form of technical support and various programs, the most notable and enduring was called *Caretakers stewardship program.*

Many years later, in 2009, as a proof of its success, the Florida Department of Agriculture and Consumer Services, the agency that regulates the pest control industry in Florida, recognized the Caretakers program with the Commissioner's Award for Pesticide Stewardship. In awarding the recognition, the Commissioner put it this way: "Caretakers is a model for how to make sure pesticides are used safely and effectively. The program is so effective that we have required other companies to follow this approach when they have registered structural fumigants."[18] The award was given fourteen years after Caretakers was first implemented and had been running continuously. By this time, the fumigant that was our competitor when I first came to Florida was no longer being used as a structural fumigant.

The other crucial component of the original Product Stewardship program was to provide better training as one of the ways we could eparate ourselves from the competition.

When I first came to work in the territory, I noticed that most fumigators were being trained by their managers or other people in the industry. Managers and others passed along good tips to new fumigators, but training varied from company to company, and sometimes bad habits were passed along with the good.

I found a great mentor in the person of Art Leasure, a veteran Dow salesman who had worked in Florida for many years before I arrived. He was well respected in the fumigation industry and had "planted good seeds" throughout his career. He also saw the wisdom of separating ourselves from competition by providing better training.

Under his leadership and masterful coordination, our Florida sales team put together a yearly training program for fumigators, which became very popular and well attended. We jokingly labeled these programs "death marches" because at the end of January, we would travel to multiple cities in South Florida in a relatively short period of time to offer the training before the busy fumigation season started. It was intensive and exhausting, but Leasure made it possible by providing superb logistic support: making arrangements with venues and hotels and hauling a trailer with all the literature, audiovisual, and demonstration equipment needed.

It is worth noting that no sales transactions actually occurred during these marches. Shortsighted critics argued that the marches did not increase product sales and only generated expenses. Looking back though, we were transitioning to a "different jungle," and with these activities, we were sowing the seed of the next phase of our training offering and marketing program, as I will describe next.

In the years that we conducted the "death marches," we started implementing a method of teaching called *show and tell*. We had demonstrations of how to use specialized equipment with actual participation by the attendants. We soon realized how effective this hands-on training was, coupled with the traditional lecture-type training. Slowly, an idea evolved in my mind, perhaps as a result of my scientific background and a model pioneered by our colleagues in California, who, in partnership with a distributor, were offering unique fumigation training.

I thought about the possibility of partnering with a teaching institution to develop a formal fumigation training program that would teach not only the methods and techniques of fumigation, but also the basic physical properties of gases. And most important, a program that would show students how to properly do fumigation by having them participate in the actual fumigation of a structure from beginning to end.

At about this time, Ellen Thoms, Ph.D., joined our sales district as a technical support and development specialist. I shared my idea with her, and she was not only supportive, but she went further and said that formal training would be good for the future of the industry and our product. One of Dr. Thoms' areas of expertise was to understand, anticipate, and comply with all the regulatory requirements to keep the product registered as a viable fumigant. She was a leader who was always ahead of the curve, "climbing tall trees." She saw things coming.

Encouraged by her support, in 1988, I approached Lois Bolton, head of the Biological Sciences Department at Broward Community College. She was very receptive and immediately saw a fit for our Structural Fumigation program within their existing Pest Control Technology program. Dr. Thoms developed the initial curriculum for a six-day systematic program, which included more than twenty hours of classroom work and sixteen hours of hands-on experience in actual fumigation. The first School of Structural Fumigation was conducted in November of 1989. It ran successfully for thirteen years at Broward Community College. Then, in 2004, with the help of Rudolf Scheffrahn, Ph.D., a professor of entomology at the University of Florida (UF), the Fumigation School moved under the auspices of the prestigious and far-reaching UF.

Although Dow did not receive any revenue from helping conduct and teach at the School—all the proceeds benefited Broward Community College and, later, the University of Florida—our endeavor nevertheless provided a powerful platform for Dow to demonstrate unequivocally its support for our product and the fumigation industry and to significantly improve the level and quality of training.

I have no doubt that in founding and supporting the Fumigation School, we changed the field of competition for the better. Around 2006, a new company with a competing fumigant came into the market. Not surprisingly, they eagerly sought to become members of the Fumigation School, providing instructors and supporting it. Thus, the fumigation industry was better for it, just as Dr. Thoms had predicted, and our product was still going strong.

I was an instructor of the Fumigation School and a member of its board until I retired in 2011. At the time of this writing, the school was getting ready to hold its thirty-sixth session. Through the years, it has trained people from all over the United States, and because of its uniqueness, it has attracted students from other parts of the world as well, notably pest control companies from Europe, which specialize in treating old churches and cathedrals whenever irreplaceable wooden ornaments and works of art get infested with beetles or termites. Using fumigation techniques, these companies have been able to completely eliminate infestations without damaging the priceless artifacts.

Other areas of instruction that the school started providing later was teaching fumigation techniques for elimination of bed bugs in residences and pests in commodities and nonresidential structures, such as mills, bakeries, and warehouses, for which our product obtained registration from the Environmental Protection Agency (EPA).

These are examples of how the school, coupled with constant efforts to adapt our offering to help solve problems in new industries, kept our product competitive and viable. More broadly, the SWOT analysis I conducted when I first moved to Florida allowed me to understand that our product had innate benefits—strengths—that justified its higher price, and it allowed me to realize that the fumigation industry in general needed better support and training—opportunities—which our company could provide, allowing us to benefit the industry and cope with the threats of increased regulation and product obsolescence.

Monopoly and Collusion

Every industry has good members, those that innovate, create new products, find ways to solve intractable problems, satisfy needs that were not met before, and, in short, have a long-term positive influence on the field in which they operate. As salespeople, we sometimes may not like our market competitors, but as the experiment of the Soviet Union proved, without good competition, innovation is stifled and eventually everyone loses. Good competitors keep us on our toes and prevent us from taking our customers for granted and vice versa.

Yet it would be naïve to pretend that all competitors are good for the industry or beneficial to consumers. The challenge lies in recognizing that some of these come actually disguised as competitors, but in reality they are not. At some point we may have to face predatory behaviors from these market entities.

Consider for a moment the following situation: let's say you own a retail store in an established neighborhood. Through good business practices and superior customer service you have developed a loyal and profitable clientele. But then, a couple of stores near you collude to lower their prices below cost with the purpose of pushing your store out of business. Understandably, you lose customers and eventually are forced to close, after which, the two stores raise their prices significantly and cut down customer service costs. The bottom line is that consumers are now worse off with your store closed.

Although it is beyond the scope of this book to dwell deeply into complex antitrust laws and regulations, as salespeople we must become familiar with these laws and be on the lookout for companies that offer prices to customers that are unrealistically low. It is incumbent upon us to seek help from technical experts and legal personnel to determine if the low pricing is the result of a technical breakthrough, a *loss-leader pricing strategy* (i.e., where a product is sold at a price below its market cost to stimulate other sales of more profitable goods or services), or a hidden ulterior motive to drive us out of business and to monopolize. Although the first two are legal, the third one is not. Offensive and defensive strategies may be necessary.

Offensively, litigation may be necessary if there is evidence of collusion or price-fixing between two or more of your competitors. Conversely, it is critically important that as a salesperson you never engage in discussions of pricing, costs, discounts, or other sensitive marketing data with your market competitors because any comment or discussion involving these subjects you have with them could be considered a violation of antitrust laws. (For more information see *Competition Counts*, a Federal Trade Commission Publication.[19])

Defensively, you may have to deploy financial programs that protect your customers and reward their loyalty. But again, these programs are hugely more effective when coupled with the principles we have discussed so far. The programs become confirmation in the eyes of your customers that you are indeed a blessing to them.

Competitive and Cooperative Thought Systems

The Fifth Principle has two directives. The first directive—to understand our competition—was amply discussed in the previous sections of this chapter and its importance cannot be overstated. Most salespersons have no difficulty in putting it to good practice. It is the second directive—to value our competition—that may become controversial and more difficult to practice. Some may even find it loathsome. In some cases, our antagonistic view of competition arises from encounters and experiences with predatory market entities disguised as competitors, as was discussed in the previous section. Understandably, these experiences ruin our view of good, legitimate competition as well. This is unfortunate because good competition is a force that compels us to innovate, to use our talents creatively, and to not take our customers for granted.

Valuing our competition requires a paradigm shift from a cold, purely competitive thought system to a cooperative thought system. Let me explain.

Our perception of what competition is begins early in life. I say "perception" because some aspects of our idea of competition are actually based on incorrect or incomplete paradigms. Competitive sports, which are designed to produce winners and losers, are most people's first encounter with competition. Then, as we go through life, we perceive ourselves competing endlessly in most of our endeavors. As students, we compete with others for grades, friendships, and popularity. We compete for the openings at better colleges. Later, we compete with other applicants to get a job. As sales professionals, we compete with other sales professionals in our field. The result is that we develop a narrow, black-and-white view of competition and see it as something we must defeat before it defeats us. We believe that unless we are winning, we must necessarily be losing.

Yet, nature shows us that arrangements with win–win outcomes are not only possible, but the only ones that are sustainable in the long run. Over eons, living things evolved through synergistic arrangements from unicellular to multicellular, to organisms, on to tribes or packs, on to societies, on to countries, and so on. But for every successful arrangement that endured, billions or perhaps trillions of arrangements lasted little or none at all. They are still happening of course, but we now understand the main ingredient of the recipe of those that are sustainable, they are win–win.

Cooperative competition within an industry in our modern world, referred to as *coopetition* is not only possible, but highly desirable. According to Wikipedia, "The concept appeared as early as 1913, being used to describe the relationships among proximate independent dealers of the Sealshipt Oyster System, who were instructed to cooperate for the benefit of the system while competing with each other for customers in the same city."

It makes sense, of course, that when competitors derive their business from the utilization of a natural resource such as oyster beds, fisheries, forests, farms, and the like, they all cooperate to keep those natural resources healthy and sustainable for the benefit of all. In fact, failing to do so would be the collective equivalent of "killing the goose that laid the golden eggs." But also, in the last three decades or so, we are slowly realizing that every industry impacts the ecosystem directly and/or indirectly. The impact is not only confined to the direct exploitation of natural resources, but it also involves the ultimate fate of the byproducts that every industry generates. Even high-tech industries generate waste byproducts which need to be recycled or properly mitigated. That is an endeavor where coopetition is becoming essential.

Many decades ago, a young engineer and friend of mine who had moved to California's Silicon Valley realized this growing need and established a company to treat air emissions and wastewater laced with heavy metals generated by the dozens of companies that were settling there and producing the integrated circuit boards or "chips" going into the myriad of electronic products that were becoming part of our lives. Over the years, he became very successful and made many innovations to his techniques as a result of cooperating, not only with the companies he serviced, but with competing companies that provide similar servicers as his. He is an ardent believer in coopetition and periodically helps his competitors solve technical issues and share innovations. This practice has been part of his success, he said, because thanks to it "we all became better at what we do."*

As mentioned previously, the creation of the School of Structural Fumigation was an example of a win–win cooperative arrangement between market competitors in the fumigation industry. But in almost every industry, we find that the establishment of trade associations and participation of competitors in such associations is truly beneficial to their members, and an invaluable vehicle to exchange technical information, provide continuous training, and "make the competitors better at what they do." Thus, the differences that inherently exist among competitors actually become a valuable resource, when used cooperatively. This is the spirit of "value your competition," the second directive of the Fifth Principle.

---

* JV Systems, Inc., Morgan Hill, CA, established in 1968

CHAPTER 6

CONQUERING HEARTBREAK HILL

"The universe operates through a dynamic exchange . . . giving and receiving are different aspects of the flow of energy in the universe. And in our willingness to give that which we seek, we keep the abundance of the universe circulating in our lives."

—Deepak Chopra

Throughout this book I have talked about energy and the laws of energy. I've postulated that Love is a form of energy and that one of the laws of energy is that we cannot create (or destroy) Love, only transform it. It is through this transformation that we create and maintain long-term business and personal relationships. Since we cannot create Love energy, it follows that we must constantly obtain it in order to function effectively as human beings; in short, we need to have a supply of it. Unless we do this, there will come a time when we will literally feel empty, wasted, or experience occupational burnout.

I am not referring here to a physical lack. You may be well nourished, in good health, and have a good income, yet still feel emotionally empty. We see this paradox becoming more and more prevalent in countries that are materially wealthy. In the lands of "milk and honey," hordes of people are emotionally hungry—more specifically Love-deprived. This is not figurative speech; it is a statement of fact.

Therefore, the Sixth Principle is what closes the loop. It is what will get us through "heartbreak hill."

So here we are, after learning and making a habit of counting our blessings, we took the long road of loving our customers. Along the way we discovered our talents, some of which with the help of other people, and learned unique ways to use them to serve the needs of our customers and to become a blessing to them. We encountered thorny roads, but also green fruitful ones, and we planted good seeds for the future while balancing planting and harvesting. We ran along many competing runners, some were faster, and some were slower, but we learned from all of them, and some learned from us. Now, a most challenging road lies ahead. This road will make us or break us. In order to succeed, we must focus on our own selves, on the question of how to continuously replenish—or better yet, how to increase our energy supply—and how to increase the efficiency of that energy.

The Sixth Principle: Practice Renewal and Multiply Your Value

The Sixth Principle is a system, a process, rather than a one-time event. It encompasses the following elements: making room for the new by releasing unproductive energy-draining elements, renewing our energy supply constantly so we can give constantly, and multiplying the value we can generate with our energy supply.

First, let's focus on the first part of the process, releasing the unproductive and energy-draining elements of our lives. This involves becoming aware of habits and thought patterns that have become obsolete or no longer serve our greater good and then taking action. Anyone who has struggled but eventually succeeded in achieving a New Year's resolution knows this is difficult—but not impossible. Although the resolution must always start within our own selves, oftentimes the actions needed to achieve lasting results require help or support from outside. I offer you a story attributed to Mahatma Gandhi to illustrate this point.

During the time that Gandhi had become a revered leader in India, a mother decided to take her son, who had the habit of consuming too much sugar, to see Gandhi and ask him if he could admonish the child into breaking his unhealthy habit. Gandhi, was affectionately called *Bapu* (spiritual father) by the people in India, and the mother truly believed that out of all people, her son would definitely listen and follow Bapu's admonition since the child greatly admired and respected him.

According to the story, the mother and child went on a long journey in order to reach Gandhi's remote retreat, or *ashram*, as it was called in India. But when they finally were able to see him and the mother requested that he admonish her son, Gandhi reflected silently and, after a while, told the mother to go home and return in two weeks. The mother left somewhat perplexed and could not fathom why Gandhi would not talk to her son right away, especially since they had travelled such a long distance.

Two weeks later, mother and son returned as requested and this time Gandhi gently but sternly admonished the boy to stop eating sugar because it was not good for his health. The boy was deeply moved by Gandhi's words, nodded obediently, and promised to do his best to stop eating sugar.

This time the mother was pleased and grateful, but out of curiosity she asked, "Bapu, why did you not talk to my son two weeks ago when we first came to see you?" Gandhi responded with a smile, "Mother, two weeks ago I too was eating too much sugar."

The moral of this story is obvious: the advice we give others is more convincing and genuine when it comes from our own mastery in overcoming a particular habit or situation, but it's also worth noticing that *both the child and Gandhi benefited from the encounter.* Even an enlightened person such as Gandhi required an outside force, in the form of an encounter with a mother and child, to modify his own habit.

Habit Modification Techniques

Much has been learned about habit-modification from a twelve-step program first introduced in 1935 by Bill Wilson and Dr. Robert Holbrook Smith, cofounders of Alcoholics Anonymous (AA). Since its birth in Akron, Ohio, the program has grown globally and has undeniably helped countless people to overcome the detrimental habit of alcoholism, which affects not only the person but also his or her relationships.

How can this program's principles be applied to the modification of other deeply engrained habits?

In fact, the development of a Personal Talent Inventory discussed in chapter 1 that has helped convicts change their thought patterns could be credited as an application of a couple of steps from the AA program.** The humble recognition that in order to change some of our habits we may require help from outside ourselves—or a

---

**Made a searching and fearless moral inventory of ourselves.*
Continued to take personal inventory, and when we were wrong, promptly admitted it.

power greater than ourselves—is engrained in at least five of the twelve steps of the AA program.

To be fair, the AA program has had its share of critics, with some of the criticism directed precisely at the program's reliance on the belief of a greater power. But many studies done since its inception have shown that the AA program has helped even agnostics and atheists to remain sober. Perhaps one of the reasons the AA program and other twelve step-programs are successful is because they use holistic principles; they recognize that not only are we made of matter and energy but also our functioning is governed by both, *whether we see the energy part or not.*

Imagine a distant sailboat moving swiftly on the surface of a lake; If we did not believe in the wind, we would miss a big portion of its reality as a sailboat. Paradoxically, even as the wind remains constant, the sailboat has the power to change direction, but *it needs the wind to do so.*

This is worth reflecting for a moment. Likewise, we have the power to change old habits, but, in order to do so, we must recognize and work with the energy that surrounds us. We don't need to understand or label what this energy is. It could be the love that is given by a support group, a force for good, the universe, or the traditional Deity.[20] Whatever it is, it is crucially important in our practice of renewal to continuously examine behaviors or thought patterns that are taking us in an unwanted direction and have become a drag on our business or personal relationships and then allow ourselves to receive support from someone or something in order to break these habits.

Moreover, *old habits*, by definition, are deeply engrained in our physical and mental fabric and will always resist furiously all attempts to be cast out; therefore, it's easier to replace them with new habits. The reason for this is that nature abhors a vacuum. If you decide to get rid of an old habit all at once and have not a compelling directive and a well-planned new habit ready to take its place, in essence you are creating a hole, a vacuum, which will make you miserable and will immediately be filled by the same old habit, albeit strengthened, or by other habits that may not necessarily be better than the previous one.

To illustrate this segment on breaking with the old and making room for the new, I would like to share an experience recounting how I was able to replace my habit of chain-smoking more than thirty-nine years ago. You will see how the principles laid out in the previous paragraphs were at work, followed by the tactics in more detail. This is how it went

After making the resolution to stop smoking, I marked a date on my calendar and prepared myself for Q-Day—the quitting day—by first writing a "Decree of Renouncement," an honest and detailed two-page document stating why I needed to stop smoking and how I was going to do it. I can't stress enough the importance of taking the time to write this document first and foremost, in your own words and in advance of the actual Q-Day.

The first part of the decree included actual physical symptoms I was experiencing that were caused by smoking:

> *I'm beginning to feel effects of smoking on my health. Pain in left side of my chest is becoming worse. My throat is always dry and tender. I have felt my heart skip a beat several times. I'm simply not very productive due to smoking. I feel tired and wasted most of the time. Smoking in the morning makes me sick, sick and nauseated. Smoking is like*

a one-way trap, the longer I smoke, the less chances I have to be able to quit successfully. I have will power, now I need determination.

The second part of the document included a clear vision of myself with the habit of smoking replaced by other healthier habits:

I picture the day when I finally will be able to be free of this vice. My lungs will be clear and my breath and teeth fresher. Hours will turn into days, days into weeks, and weeks into months and years. Years of cigarette-free living! Without headaches or fuzzy thinking, or hands shaking in the morning . . . Without this vague, bothersome pain in my left side. I see myself at age fifty, running or playing tennis, slender, dynamic, active.

The final part was a formal pledge. It sealed my commitment and its gravity, and it called for help from a greater power:

Due to the above reasons and to many others, including expense; how smoke stinks my car, my room; how it bothers other people's right to breath clean air; how it is affecting my health and how it will undoubtedly inflict irreparable damage and future suffering, etc. etc., I, Rodolfo E. Subieta, hereby declare and renounce of my own free will and conviction the habit of smoking cigarettes either for pleasure or out of psychological need, or out of a need of a feeling to "join" other smokers, either strangers, friends, or partners down the path of this unhealthy habit. I also declare that I will put forth a fight and hereby declare war on my habit of smoking and will resist the need, as it will surely arise, and the temptation to go back once the need is gone; that I will not save any resources, nor will I go into this war half-committed, but I will use the best of my abilities and will never be caught off guard, until this habit of mine is forever banished, which is never. This document pledges myself and my word as a man of honor to this worthy and life-saving cause. So help me God.

If you find the above document somewhat familiar and resembling the Declaration of Independence, you are correct. In many ways it was my declaration of independence from a tyrannical habit, and I needed an inspiring document with universal principles and proven track record. Writing these down is crucially important because when Q-Day comes and you are hit by the first wave of cravings like with a ton of bricks, you need to have your document handy and ready to refresh your memory of all the reasons why you are quitting. When you are in the midst of withdrawal pangs, it's easy to rationalize that you really don't need to quit. You need powerful, compelling arguments and a reminder that you are not alone; *the wind is out there blowing, and you're changing directions.*

If you can resist the first wave of cravings, the second wave will be less intense, the third even less, and so on. If you can get through the first day, the second day will be easier. It also helps to pick a Q-Day when you can be reasonably free of stress and avoid things that you associate with the particular habit. In my case, I picked a weekend and avoided coffee because I associated drinking a cup of coffee with smoking. Therefore, I switched to tea for a while, which provided me with some caffeine, so that I did not have to deal with double cravings. To help fill the void created by not smoking, I also started jogging, taking long walks, and playing soccer and tennis. I was able to replace my habit of smoking with those healthier activities, and after thirty-nine years, I can still perform and enjoy those activities with the exception of soccer, which I gave up after spraining an ankle.

I believe the theory and practical steps provided in the previous paragraphs can be applied to replacing other habits that you deem detrimental or energy-draining. In addition to being grateful to Emotions Anonymous, another twelve-step program, I also join millions of people in gratitude to Thomas Jefferson for writing such a profoundly transformational and lasting document as the Declaration of Independence, which helped inspire the original thirteen colonies into changing their course and, by so doing, into becoming the United States of America. The principles laid out in that document are as useful today as they were in 1776.

Reasons Why Relationships Wither or Die

There are many similarities between keeping a long, productive business relationship and a long, happy marriage. In both, one must continuously pour energy in the form of Love. In a marriage, Love is the fuel that our souls need to get up every morning and face the challenges of the world. You can't love and encourage your partner for only one day, one week, or even one month and expect that love will feed his or her soul for a year. Indifference is not what we need. Indifference is not energy. When we feel empty, ignored, or taken for granted, we may survive or tolerate the situation for a while, but eventually we will have to look for fulfillment somewhere else. Often in the case of couples, when this happens, they start distancing from one another and looking for fulfillment at work, in a cause, or with another partner. Our bodies cannot survive long on yesterday's bread, nor our souls thrive on yesterday's love.

In business relationships, we may have a handful of loyal customers that religiously buy from us and do not demand much. We may have done good deeds for them in the past, but then we make the mistake of thinking that because of this, we deserve their business forever, we take them for granted. We invest all our energy on other demanding customers because the adage which says "the squeaky wheel gets the grease" is true; so, one day, we are faced with the unpleasant reality that our loyal customer has started buying from our competitor. When this happens, our first reaction will probably be to curse our competitor, but this may be a good time to take inventory of the things that made you lovable with this customer in the first place and whether or not you stopped doing them—more specifically, when did you stop being a blessing to him or her?

But then, there are also situations when you realize the values and practices of a customer simply are incompatible with yours or your company's, or such values have become incompatible due to a change in ownership or management. This is the subject of our next section.

Detrimental Behaviors and Losing Propositions

In Kahlil Gibran's masterpiece *The Prophet*, a merchant asks Almustafa, the mystic sage, to provide wisdom on "Buying and Selling." The beloved sage responds like this:

> To you the earth yields her fruit, and you shall not want if you but know how to fill your hands.It is in exchanging the gifts of the earth that you shall find abundance and be satisfied.

> Yet unless the exchange be in love and kindly justice, it will but lead some to greed and others to hunger.

Consider for a moment the following situations: Let's say you own a retail store and a person comes into your store to shoplift; is this person a customer?

Your quick answer may be, "Of course not, he didn't come to buy; he's only a thief."

All right, what about a person that comes into your store and then switches the price tags of merchandise and pays lower for a more expensive item. Now, is he a customer? After all, he did buy from you.

These situations are clearly illegal and easier to discern in retail or short-term sales. However, situations parallel to these do arise in some long-term business relationships, except that they are more ambiguous and more difficult to discern quickly. As salespeople whose business depends on long-term relationships, how can we make sense out of these seemingly conflicting realities that a customer may actually be a losing proposition, that our exchanges with this customer are not "in kindly justice," or perhaps that we are confronting a predatory entity? And most important, how do we deal effectively with these situations?

First, I will turn to evolutionary biology for insights on why these entities exist, and from this platform of understanding provide further insights on how to adjust, manage, and overcome them.

Early on in our evolutionary history, some unicellular organisms started aggregating randomly with other unicellular organisms in the ocean. A few of these unions actually turned into win–win synergistic cooperative arrangements and evolved into more complex multicellular organisms, capable of surviving and thriving more effectively in their environment. Notice the wisdom of this natural force: *organisms capable of cooperating with each other in win–win synergistic arrangements were rewarded by becoming better users of resources available.* Yet, the evolutionary progression was neither straightforward nor easy. Billions of arrangements never succeeded because they were either not win–win (one organism just took over the other) or were not synergistic (they did not make the combined organism any better than either one alone). In either case, the aggregated organism did not gain a lasting advantage. In many cases, the combined organism actually became less capable and more lethargic than either of its original components.

This phenomenon is worth noting because it also manifests itself at the macro level—for example, in personal and business relationships, in corporation mergers, and in aggregations among tribes, kingdoms, states, and countries. There are relationships, for instance, that actually become detrimental to one or both parties. The same thing occurs to corporations that become less competitive and lose value after a merger.

In this elegant laboratory of the universe, we observe that certain patterns become replicated from the microscopic level, up to the organic and societal level, and continue all the way up to the astronomic level. This is the fascinating field of fractal theory. We find that what works at the unicellular level also works at the societal level, that in order for the new aggregated entity to become sustainably more effective, the relationship must be a *synergistic win–win cooperative arrangement.*

Notice how this principle is at work in the functioning of our own bodies. We coexist with trillions of bacteria that live in our digestive system. They help us digest and absorb nutrients and produce some vitamins that are essential to our health and survival. In return, our bodies provide the bacteria with harborage and raw nutrients. Yet, we also know that a relatively small number of species of bacteria, the ones we call *pathogens*, are capable of making us sick and even killing us. That is a lesson from nature that cannot be ignored and has profound implications in the development of personal or business long-term relationships.

During my sales career, I came to deal with a very small number of "customers" that run their business affairs clearly in a pathological manner. Either due to ignorance, greed, or both, these individuals operated from a paradigm that only included, "I must win, and I will win, and I don't give a damn who loses." The realization was not as immediate as when you catch somebody shoplifting or switching price tags in your store; but in the course of business interactions with these individuals, it became clear that to continue to deal with them would be detrimental to our own business. As it happens, it's easier to get into these lose–win relationships than to cut them off. This is often the case when we come into a new unfamiliar territory and we are ignorant of the backgrounds of all its members. We are understandably eager to show progress by increasing our customer base and revenue, so we enter into these relationships to our later regret. In other cases, we may either inherit these business relationships from our predecessor, or due to a change in their ownership, the relationship transforms from a win–win to a lose–win. But, regardless of how it came to be, when it becomes imperative to sever the business relationship, you must make the case to your upper management that the revenue provided by these buyers is not worth the long-term damage they could inflict to your business and to the industry.

Again, I was fortunate that in my particular experience, my upper managers were not only supportive of severing these relationships, but actually put in place a well-defined process, backed by our legal department, to "stop sales" of our product to companies that were unwilling or unable to use the product according to label directions or that committed infractions documented by the regulatory agency. The process included periodic and meticulous inspections, documentation, and coordination with regulatory agencies to make sure the process had no loopholes and that it was legal, timely, fair, and warranted.

Severing detrimental business relationships is part of the renewal process. It's never easy, but it's a critically important part of long-term account management. It should never be carried out hastily in ignorance, or as an act of reprisal, but as a surgical method performed with precision and ample knowledge of the reasons, risks, and consequences that such a procedure will cause.

When done correctly, it is a liberating experience, described by Covey as "win–win or no deal." I have found in my own experience that when we approached and performed the severing as a good surgical team does, our business did not suffer. Instead, our credibility and loyalty among other customers increased, as they realized that, by our actions, we were protecting not only our business but the industry that was so dear to them as well.

Now that we have discussed the phase of the renewal process dealing with releasing energy-draining elements from our lives and from our business relationships, we are ready to discuss other phases, always keeping in mind that although we discuss them separately as a matter of necessity, they need not be practiced separately, as they all form part of a continuum. In order to illustrate the whole process, I would like to share the following parable with you.

A Parable: The Village Where It Never Rained

> Long time ago in a not-so-far-away land, there was a small village. The people who lived there were isolated from the rest of the world by very tall mountains, and they had a very peculiar no-

tion about water. For one, it never rained there, and there was only one well in the whole village, which was under the control of the village's priesthood. The high priest of the village was the ultimate authority regarding who got water and how much. People who broke the rules established by the priesthood were punished by having their water rations withheld. Since water deprivation was an accepted way of punishment in this society, parents also felt that it was right and proper to discipline their children by depriving them of water. Some of these children grew up and became priests, who in turn used thirst as means of punishing and demonstrating their "power" to others.

Through time, this system resulted in a mentality of water scarcity that permeated this whole society. Individuals would hoard water in all kinds of containers and would hide them because they were convinced that there was not enough for everyone. Frequently, the water in these containers became stale, unwholesome, or contaminated. People who drank this stale water became ill. But because of their strong scarcity mentality, they thought that it was "normal" to become a little ill, that pain was sometimes the price they had to pay for quenching their thirst! They accepted it as a way of life and thought nothing wrong about trading or giving each other unwholesome water. Men grudgingly gave their wives small rations of stale water, and mothers gave even smaller rations to their children, who fought among themselves and grew up resentful of their siblings because they thought that every drop of water their brothers got was water they could have gotten instead. And everyone was thirsty, but also afraid of drinking water and getting sick.

And the people thought they had no choice.

One day, a young maiden decided to take a journey to the tall mountains that surrounded the village. Her parents and villagers considered her a "tomboy" and most of the time she felt she did not quite fit in this society. The priests had warned that the mountains were the dwelling place of souls in penance and that according to legends and ancient scrolls, people who went to the mountains never returned; so the villagers never ventured there, much less alone. At dawn, this young woman set on her journey climbing the mountain to a considerable height. The evening came and she slept on a ledge. She had strange dreams in which she heard different voices giving her conflictive advice. "You will perish. Go back to the village and conform," one voice would say. "Go on. You will find what you are looking for," another voice said.

The following morning, she continued to climb the mountain. As the sun was setting on the second day of her journey, she reached a small valley, and in the distance she saw the sun's reflection on the surface of something very bright and immense. That night, with her provision of water exhausted, she slept peacefully despite the thirst. At about noon on the third day, she reached a beautiful plateau from which she could see the whole village down in the distance. Instead of souls in penance, she also saw a vast lake with crystal-clear water that was being fed by melting snow from the peaks high above. Almost to the point of exhaustion, she drank from the lake. As the cool water went inside her, she immediately noticed the difference between this water and the stale water she had drank all her life down in the village. It felt so marvelously fresh and soothing. For the first time in her life, she drank and drank and drank without measure, until her thirst was finally quenched. She felt light and renewed. "What kind of water is this, that makes me feel so?" she asked, "Where does it come from?" She explored the surroundings and discovered that the water in this lake was constantly being replenished. It received water in the form of melting snow from above and fed many springs. It dawned on her that the reason why this lake was so fresh and beautiful was because it gave as it received. She started laughing softly at first, then gradually louder and louder until her laughter reverberated throughout the mountains creating ripples on the water; and for a moment it seemed that the mountains, the lake, and everything around her was laughing with her . . . vibrating and rolling with the joy of Oneness.

As two priests were taking their morning stroll toward the village's square, they noticed a gathering of people. They were listening to the woman talk. She was radiant and was telling the crowd about the "inexhaustible source of water" that she had found and was available to them. If they could only believe and follow her, she could show them the way. Some villagers shook their heads, whispering to each other, "The wench's gone mad, there's no such thing as unlimited water. Water is scarce, it's always been, it always will be." But others listened and were intrigued by the words of this woman, who spoke with such authority. The two priests reported to the high priest what they heard. He listened with great concern because he knew that his hold on power was being threatened.

The word spread throughout the village that someone had found an inexhaustible source of water and that some had followed this person and found it to be true. These people had been transformed and were in turn telling others. They spoke with joy in their voices and gave people to drink freely the water they brought from the Source. They said that the Source was available to everyone, and that it was always so. They even said that the well in the village, controlled by the priests, was fed underground by the same Source above. Some people believed; some were confused. The priests were not happy and decided to take action.

The high priest decreed that anyone caught going to the mountains or even spreading rumors about the high water source would be tried as a "heretic" and cutoff from his water rations. Also, some villagers who had been hoarding water were afraid their hoard would become worthless if people started going straight to the Source. One of them decided to infuse some of his hoarded water with a toxic plant and gave it away anonymously as "water from the high source." Those who drank it became very ill and a few died. The priests used this as evidence to discredit the water from the high source and to persecute those who gave it away or talked about it. Other villagers, who had grown accustomed to using water as means of retaining control and authority over others, welcomed this latest development, and became staunch defenders of the limited-water status quo.

Even to this date, the people in the village are using water as means to gain power and control. But some remember or are told about the young maiden who spoke of the Inexhaustible Source. She no longer lives there. Throughout the years, many have taken the journey up the mountain and found the Inexhaustible Source. Fulfilling the village's legends and ancient scrolls, they have never returned to the village. They have settled on the valleys on the other side of the mountain, where water from the Source flows freely and is allowed to reach every person that abides there.[21]

The Three Bewares

Although renewal is a natural process, the practice of *seeking renewal* does not happen spontaneously. It requires commitment and effort on our part and an understanding of the forces that can block its process. Hopefully, the simple parable helped you recognize three human tendencies that get in the way and are extremely counterproductive to our practice of renewal. I call these tendencies the *Three Bewares*:

1. *Beware of hoarding and hoarders.* Hoarding arises from a deeply ingrained belief that

resources are scarce; therefore, we believe we need to accumulate them. This accumulation actually validates scarcity and makes it real. It creates more scarcity, which in turn generates more hoarding. In essence, the free flow of the resource is stopped. Hoarding actually disconnects us from our source. Hoarding is different from receiving, using, transforming, and giving, which are what produces synergy that benefits both the giver and the receiver.

2. ***Beware of using a resource as means to gain power and control over others.*** We may mistakenly believe that we can use Love in this fashion. "I will only love you if you do this or that." This is a subtle but very common practice. It can become a habit that people use unconsciously because they learned it as children and never questioned its validity. It isn't Love what is being given or withheld; it's usually affection or attention, but as children we crave these things like we crave candy. Parents dangle their affection in front of their children like a carrot in front of a donkey. Then we grow up thinking that this was Love—or "tough love." This is not effective or sustainable because those who are at the receiving

end of this practice eventually realize they are being manipulated and will either resent it or sever the relationship altogether.

3. ***Beware of self-proclaimed gatekeepers of Love energy.*** These gatekeepers can be people or systems. They institutionalize the flow of a free resource and set themselves as the brokers of the resource. They embody the two previous tendencies combined. They can and do succeed for a while until their subjects realize they can go to the source themselves.

The Multiplication of Value

Lastly, as part of our practice of renewal, we must learn to use our time and energy supply in ways that exponentially increase its reach and effectiveness. Because as someone once rightfully observed, "No matter how good our intentions and physical strength, and no matter how many times we try, we simply cannot get to the moon by jumping."

As stated in a previous chapter, Stephen Covey argues that all things are created twice. The first creation occurs in the mind. This is the idea, the blueprint. Although the first creation is crucial, value is not realized until the second creation occurs. Value is what all salespeople must ultimately create and deliver.

In the end, the exercise of an action is what defines all things in the universe. Even inanimate objects are defined in terms of what they "do." An archway built over a river becomes a bridge only because it "bridges" two shores. Its value as a bridge is not realized until it acts as a bridge. The blueprint of a bridge, although an important step in its development, offers absolutely no value to those who want to cross to the other shore. Likewise, an apple seed represents the first creation. If the seed is not acted upon—planted—multiplication does not occur.

The multiplication of value in nature is always the result of energy put in action utilizing a principle known as *leveraging.*

I'd like to introduce to you one of the greatest mathematicians, scientists, and inventors of all times. His name was Archimedes. He was born in the year 287 BC in Syracuse, Sicily. At that time Syracuse was an independent Greek city-state with a five hundred-year history.

Archimedes is credited with the discovery and further application of a simple mechanical device called a *lever*, which allows a force to be amplified. There is a quote attributed to

Archimedes that says, "Give me a lever long enough and a place to stand, and I will move the earth." The people of Syracuse used Archimedes' mechanical inventions built upon the principle of leveraging very effectively in the defense of their land when it was attacked by the Romans. Here's an account of the event.

> When, therefore, the Romans assaulted the walls in two places at once, fear and consternation stupefied the Syracusans, believing that nothing was able to resist that violence and those forces. But when Archimedes began to ply his engines, he at once shot against the [Roman] land forces all sorts of missile weapons, and immense masses of stone that came down with incredible noise and violence; against which no man could stand; for they knocked down those upon whom they fell in heaps, breaking all their ranks and files. In the meantime huge poles thrust out from the walls over the ships sunk some by the great

weights which they let down from on high upon them; others they lifted up into the air by an iron hand or beak like a crane's beak and, when they had drawn them up by the prow, and set them on end upon the poop, they plunged them to the bottom of the sea; or else the ships, drawn by engines within, and whirled about, were dashed against steep rocks that stood jutting out under the walls, with great destruction of the soldiers that were aboard them. A ship was frequently lifted up to a great height in the air (a dreadful thing to behold), and was rolled to and fro, and kept swinging, until the mariners were all thrown out, when at length it was dashed against the rocks, or let fall.[22]

Keep in mind that the Archimedes' "engines" that are so graphically described in the account above were muscle-powered. No diesel or electricity was available at that time. Archimedes himself was not too enthusiastic to build such war engines. Plutarch, his biographer, writes that Archimedes was persuaded to do so only because his friend King Hiero asked him to do so. It is a sad fact that most scientific discoveries find their way into war applications, but again, natural forces are intrinsically neither good nor bad, they simply are.

The principle and power of leveraging discovered by Archimedes is found all around nature; but then, people also learned that it could be applied to the areas of business and finance. Middle-class people achieved homeownership by leveraging a small down payment and steady income with a mortgage from a financial institution. Leveraged buyouts of large corporations became popular in the 1980s.

Lastly, the advent of the internet, with all its platforms including social media, email, web pages, blogs, messaging, and more, has become one of the most powerful leveraging devices of modern times. The internet has made it possible for any individual with access to it to transform basically any human discipline and enterprise including commerce, marketing, banking, entertainment, journalism, transportation, communications, and even medicine and politics into something else—for good or bad. The internet is still evolving at a fast pace, and it is safe to predict that it will affect every aspect of our lives. However, let's not lose sight of its origins and the fact that it is only a leveraging device. It still requires someone or something to provide an input for that input to be amplified and multiplied. And most important, the internet does not and cannot abolish the law of gravity or the laws of thermodynamics nor any of the natural laws of the universe we have discussed. It is to our benefit that we learn to use it wisely.

Here is a sample list of the principle of leveraging at work (that may or may not involve the internet):

1. It is used by an apple seed, which using small resources of its own, leverages the energy of the sun into creating an apple tree out of minerals, air, and water.
2. It is used by a couple who, using a small capital of their own, opens up a business. Then, using this capital and their labor, they leverage the resources of financial institutions to grow into a large enterprise that employs hundreds of people.
3. Leveraging is used by a teacher, who trains other trainers.

4. Leveraging is achieved by word-of-mouth advertising.
5. Leveraging is achieved when your actions in the marketplace cause your customers to refer you to other potential customers.
6. Leveraging is achieved by adding your talents to the talents of others in your team to create powerful waves in the marketplace that you alone could not possibly make.

In short, leveraging is the masterful multiplication of your talents, which allows you to increase your efficiency exponentially to literally move mountains, if you endeavor to do so. When this is done in concert with the principles presented in this book, you become a powerful and sustainable source of blessings to your customers and others.

To summarize, looking now at the whole picture, practicing renewal consists of four activities not necessarily in this same order:

One, making room for the new, by questioning obsolete paradigms and habits; replacing them with good ones; recognizing detrimental entities and, in some cases, surgically severing business relationships that may have become losing propositions and are causing prohibitive drains on your energy supply.

Two, finding and staying connected to your source of primordial energy and staying gratefully receptive to the blessings that come your way or others offer you.

Three, becoming aware of human tendencies, systems, and institutions that block your practice of renewal.

And four, transforming your energy in creative ways and multiplying its value so that you in turn can efficiently bring blessings to your customers and others with who you want to keep long-term relationships.

In our practice of renewal, nature can be an excellent teacher to the marathon salesperson. There's probably no more beautiful example of the renewal process as the passing of the seasons: Leaves fall from trees in autumn to nurture the earth below. During the resting period late in the fall and winter, the soil replenishes its energy in order to make plants bloom in the spring. And, in the spring and summer, we see the visible benefits of what happened in the fall and winter. Would it not be shortsighted to believe that spring or summer is more important, more necessary, than winter or fall? Yet in business we sometimes make the mistake to focus only on the fruit—the sale—that is usually delivered in late spring or summer, but we may totally or partially neglect the replenishing work that must take place within our sales practices and ourselves. Basically, we want eternal spring; we want to shortcut the renewal process. Like a perpetual motion machine, this violates natural laws and is, therefore, unsustainable in the long run.

Thus, the Sixth Principle is what will get us through the heartbreak hills of our marathon sales journey.

BY WAY OF CLOSING

As we come to the end of this book, I hope the material that I presented—along with examples from science, history, business, and personal experience on how to use the six principles—will provide you with a roadmap to more effective and sustainable business practices and relationships with customers. If you have read this far, you probably realize that although this is a business book, the principles are universal and can be applied to personal relationships as well.

As a testimony, I must confess that writing this book has been a humbling as well as a learning experience for me. One of the central principles of the book is the all-pervading role Love plays in so many areas of our lives, including customer relationships. In my search for ways to explain what Love is and does, I found myself researching, reading books, and taking journeys that in many ways have changed my own paradigm of what I found Love to be, *the primordial energy of the universe.*

One thing I can say with certainty is that I am still a student of Love, and now I'm even more in awe of its immensity. In many ways, I feel like an explorer, who having been born in the mountains, undertakes a marathon journey, and after countless days of travel through hills and valleys, finally arrives at the shore of an ocean, only to realize he can only glimpse at the magnitude of what is yet to be discovered.

Epilogue

As the road ahead extends and disappears,
By the misty finish line fixed in your mind's eye,
Feel the ground beneath your feet,
Supporting and propelling your stride,
And at that moment,
May you realize and start counting
The rich blessings that enfold you,
Through your marathon sales journey.

May you love your customers and be loved by them.
May your travels be fruitful and safe,
Your sushi fresh, and your coffee strong,
And always exceed your sales plans.

May your presentations be mesmerizing,
And be proud of the goods you sell,
But never be arrogant.

May you greet every new day with hope,
And every sunset with the satisfaction,
Of a goal accomplished,
A sales call made,
A relationship strengthened,
A good seed planted,
A problem solved,
An opportunity seized,
A customer's need satisfied.

May you find the time to celebrate your triumphs,
And learn from your fellow competitors.
May you gain their respect,
And value their contributions.

May you realize that time is all we've got,
But time can be on our side,
Only if we make time our friend; so,
May time be your true friend.

And as the grains of sand drop one by one,
In the hourglass of your life,
May your spirit be constantly renewed,
And may you find your cup to be,
A fountain.

—R. E. S.

NOTES

1. Wikipedia, "Newton's Law of Universal Gravitation," *Wikipedia, The Free Encyclopedia*, https://en.wikipedia. org/w/index.php?title=Newton%27s_law_of_universal_ gravitation&oldid=904495346 (accessed July 15, 2019).

2. Napoleon Hill, *The Master-Key to Riches* (New York: Fawcett Crest Books, 1965), p. 189.

3. M. Scott Peck, M.D., *In Search of Stones: A Pilgrimage of Faith, Reason, and Discovery* (New York: Hyperion, 1995), p. 367.

4. Stephen R. Covey, *The 7 Habits of Highly Effective People: Powerful Lessons in Personal Change* (New York: Simon & Schuster, 1989), p. 123.

5. Og Mandino, *A Better Way to Live: Og Mandino's Own Personal Story of Success Featuring 17 Rules to Live By* (New York and Toronto: Bantam Books, 1991), p. 53.

6. Kelly Isola, "I Am Blessed," Courage to Imagine (Unity Booklet, 2018), p. 12.

7. Covey, *The 7 Habits*, p. 99.

8. Ibid, pp. 79–80.

9. Bill Sharp, "Dow Chemical Professional Selling Seminar" (Student Workbook, Percon, 1984), pp. 50–51.

10. Leigh Buchanan, "In Praise of Selflessness: Why the Best Leaders Are Servants," *Inc. Magazine* (May 2007), pp. 33–35.

11. Uri Shulevitz, *The Treasure* (New York: Farrar, Straus and Giroux, 1978).

12. Spencer Johnson, M.D., and Larry Wilson, *The One Minute Sales Person* (New York: William Morrow and Company, Inc., 1984), pp. 17, 86.

13. Quoted from a PowerPoint presentation/workshop Sid Funk and I prepared for salespeople of Dow AgroSciences, 2011.

14. Covey, *The 7 Habits*, pp. 52–54.

15. Thomas A. Kinney, *The Carriage Trade: Making Horse-Drawn Vehicles in America* (Baltimore and London: The Johns Hopkins University Press, 2004).

16. Dawson Church, Ph.D., "The Power of a New Thought," *Unity Magazine* (September/October 2020), p. 13.

17. Covey, *The 7 Habits*, p. 101.

18. "Dow AgroSciences Receives Florida Commissioner's Stewardship Award," *CPCO Advantage* (February 2010), p. 20.

19. Federal Trade Commission, "Competition Counts: How Consumers Win When Businesses Compete" (Washington, DC: Federal Trade Commission, May 2015), https://www.ftc.gov/system/files/attachments/competition-counts/pdf-0116_competition-counts.pdf.

20. *Emotions Anonymous* (Saint Paul, Minnesota: Emotions Anonymous International, 1978), p. 2.

21. Rodolfo Subieta, Excerpt from "Letters to My Daughters on Love and Marriage" (2000).

22. John Dryden, trans., "Marcellus by Plutarch," The Internet Classics Archive, http://classics.mit.edu/Plutarch/marcellu.html.